I wish there wasn't a need
And you won't find one th
encouragement page for pa

Michelle Donnelly's facility with language; as a pastor, I appreciate her insight into the spiritual dynamics of abuse; and as a Christian, I rejoice in the fact that so many victims of abuse can be forewarned, equipped, strengthened, and delivered from their abusers. The level of wisdom and insight was nothing short of astonishing to me. Michelle lays bare the motivations, manipulations, and common tactics of abusers. Pastors, friends, counselors, and of course the abused will all be fortified, blessed, and equipped by reading this seminal work on abuse. In a word, I found this book to be nothing less than brilliant.

Gary Thomas
Author of *Sacred Marriage* and *When to Walk Away*

• • •

With the compassion and wisdom of a trusted and invested mentor, Michelle Donnelly leads readers on a gentle journey of healing from abuse and abandonment. Anchored in biblical truth and bolstered by the author's own experiences, *Safe Haven* provides exactly what the title promises: a safe place for weary, confused, and broken hearts to find help and transcendent hope.

Teasi Cannon
Speaker; author of *My Big Bottom Blessing* and *Lord, Where's My Calling?*; contributing author of *Mama Bear Apologetics: Empowering Your Kids to Challenge Cultural Lies*

• • •

Since the serpent gaslighted Eve, God has truly hated abuse. This resource can expedite years of therapy and months of healing. With Michelle Donnelly, explore examples of what to do and what not to do, and implement principles that give yourself and those you care about the precious gift of emotional and relational wholeness. When your happily ever after doesn't turn out as you hoped, Michelle Donnelly assures that you are not alone.

PeggySue Wells
Bestselling author of 30 books including *The 10 Best Decisions a Single Mom Can Make*

SAFE haven

A Devotional for the Abused
and Abandoned

MICHELLE DONNELLY

TESTIMONY

MEDIA GROUP

Safe Haven: A Devotional for the Abused and Abandoned

Copyright © 2022

Published by Testimony Media Group
Published with the assistance of The Wayne Hastings Co., LLC

All rights reserved. No part of this publication may be reproduced, distributed, or transmitted in any form or by any means, including photocopying, recording, or other electronic or mechanical methods, without the prior written permission of the publisher, except in the case of brief quotations embodied in critical reviews and certain other noncommercial uses permitted by copyright law.

Unless otherwise noted, all Scripture quotations are taken from the Holy Bible, New International Version®, NIV®. Copyright © 1973, 1978, 1984, 2011 by Biblica, Inc.® Used by permission of Zondervan. All rights reserved worldwide. www.zondervan.com. The "NIV" and "New International Version" are trademarks registered in the United States Patent and Trademark Office by Biblica, Inc.®

Scripture quotations marked BSB are taken from the Holy Bible, Berean Study Bible, BSB. Copyright © 2016, 2018 by Bible Hub. Used by permission. All rights reserved worldwide.

Scripture quotations marked ESV are taken from the ESV ® Bible (The Holy Bible, English Standard Version®). Copyright © 2001 by Crossway, a publishing ministry of Good News Publishers. Used by permission. All rights reserved.

Scripture quotations marked NLT are taken from the Holy Bible, New Living Translation. Copyright © 1996, 2004, 2015 by Tyndale House Foundation. Used by permission of Tyndale House Ministries, Carol Stream, Illinois 60188. All rights reserved.

*To my Rescuer and Redeemer:
my rescue in this life is but a glimpse
of my rescue in eternity.*

CONTENTS

Introduction 1

Section 1: The Hurt 9
    Chapter 1: God Hates Abuse..18
    Chapter 2: Jesus Knows..22
    Chapter 3: The Gaslighting of Eve 27
    Chapter 4: Separating from the Source 32
    Chapter 5: Can They Change?...38
    Chapter 6: It's Not Your Fault 44
    Chapter 7: It's Not Personal 49

Section 2: The Hiding Place..55
    Chapter 8: Why Did This Happen? 60
    Chapter 9: No Escape 66
    Chapter 10: Facing Forward 72
    Chapter 11: Boundaries..76
    Chapter 12: The Freedom of Forgiveness 81
    Chapter 13: Dealing with Discard 88
    Chapter 14: Responding in Honor.....................................92

Section 3: The Healing..97
    Chapter 15: Dad 105
    Chapter 16: Release to Receive 110
    Chapter 17: Shaming the Shame 114
    Chapter 18: I Am Who You Say I Am 119
    Chapter 19: Vision and Division 124
    Chapter 20: The Discomfort of Deliverance....................129
    Chapter 21: All Things New..134

Notes..138

INTRODUCTION

*They cried out to the L*ORD *in their trouble, and he brought them out of their distress. He stilled the storm to a whisper; the waves of the sea were hushed. They were glad when it grew calm, and he guided them to their desired haven.*
PSALM 107:28–30

It was my dream home.

In the last year of my marriage, my then husband and I hand-selected the fixtures and finishes of the semi-custom "forever" home we'd commissioned to be built. It was a farmhouse-style abode, nestled among towering box elder and redbud trees, with a trickling stream playfully lapping at the property line. It was the largest piece of property we'd ever owned, and after living in the sun-scorched Southwest, the lush Tennessee bluegrass seemed to beckon our three children, coaxing them from behind the walls of our home to explore its limitless potential for adventures.

As for the house itself, the charcoal-gray exterior gave it a sturdy, almost reverent presence in a neighborhood dappled with cheery, white-painted brick homes. But its solemn fortitude was softened by the inclusion of a Pinterest-worthy, robin's egg blue front door.

INTRODUCTION

Months before I'd ever walk through that ever-so-inviting front door, I had pored over dozens of Sherwin-Williams paint swatches to choose that "just right" shade. I finally selected Moody Blue, a vibrant shade of light blue with just a hint of ash to complement the home's gray facade.

We moved cross-country in early spring, leaving the desert Southwest for the rolling hills of Tennessee. When I walked into the home for the first time, I was in awe. Every detail of this home had been carefully curated, just as every facet of our lives had been. As we unpacked, our professionally styled family photos (with expertly coordinated but never matching outfits) eventually lined the hallways. Our spacious closets were stocked with rows of on-trend clothes. We looked the part, but in truth, the ties that bound us had been unraveling for years.

Just weeks after I first walked through my perfectly painted, dearly adored front door, our dream home became the setting of a full-scale nightmare. Within those walls I uncovered infidelity. Deceit. Betrayal. Shouts and sobs filled the rooms of this once pristine home. I wish I could tell you this was an anomaly in our relationship, but if I'm being honest, this wasn't the first time a new "forever home" had borne witness to our stormy confrontations. In a moment of clarity, I realized there was nothing left. This marriage was over.

I asked him to leave. There I stood, suddenly a thirty-five-year-old single mother of three with no friends or family for thousands of miles. The dreams I had—for our children, the marriage ministry I'd hoped we'd start—all vanished in an instant. As I stared into the bewildered faces of my brokenhearted children,

I remember dejectedly saying to God, "So, what are You going to do with me now?"

During those early days, He gently replied, *I'm making all things new.*

I received the home in the divorce settlement and had fully intended to stay there. But after the first six months (and a little bit of healing), I felt a stirring in my soul to sell the home and move to a smaller property nearby. I knew just why I couldn't stay. This house was the remnant of a dream that had died, an artifact of my broken heart.

I began cleaning the house, preparing it for showing. Just before I listed the home, I sat in the dark one evening and had an honest conversation with God about the future. I told Him, "I know it's good for me to leave this place behind, but I really do love my home."

He whispered sweetly to my heart, *Where I am taking you, you won't think about this place.*

The house sold quickly. The moving crew was a devoted band of friends and family God had assembled during my separation to bolster my children and me in this new season. And when the last box had been stowed and made ready for transport, I closed that beloved front door for the last time.

My emotions were tangled, but not in the way you'd expect. I didn't cry. I didn't get nostalgic. I didn't even bring the can of Moody Blue I had left over to paint the front door on my new-to-me home. God had already promised something good was ahead, and I was willing to follow Him on the adventure.

My children and I moved into a charming, ranch-style bungalow set in an older neighborhood on the other side of town.

INTRODUCTION

Within weeks we unpacked. Somehow this unfamiliar dwelling already possessed that unmistakable sense of "home." One early spring morning, I asked God, "What is this I'm feeling, Lord? What is different about this place?"

He whispered again to my heart, *Here you are safe. You've never been abused here before.* At those words, I wept. I rejoiced. Through this move, through this divorce, I had no way of perceiving what I truly needed to start over. But God did. He knew I needed a safe haven.

In the time since I moved, the house has been a haven of healing for my children and me. We've enjoyed sticky s'mores over backyard bonfires and cuddled under cozy blankets for double feature movie nights. But more than that, we've poured our hearts out to God in the form of desperate, late-night prayers and have experienced His redeeming grace through heartfelt, reconciling embraces. Within the walls of this home we've blossomed, and God continues to fill its halls and our hearts with His new dreams.

While God provided this place of shelter for my children and me, over time it became clear that my home was meant to be a physical representation of a spiritual reality—that God is our safe haven. He's called me by name, rescued my heart from the oppression of abuse, and drawn me under His protective compassion. And as He has tended to my wounds so fastidiously, I've learned to trust Him in a way that has brought my spirit and soul the liberty I've always longed for. God has gently revealed to me what it is to be held—to be safe—with all that I am, and I know the same is possible for you too.

INTRODUCTION

When you've been abused, it often feels as if there's no safe place—not your mind, your heart, or even your own body. Feeling unsafe in the depths of your own being is unnerving and horrifying, and the anguish and confusion that ensue can leave you feeling lost and alone.

But in it all, God is not silent or absent. Psalm 12:5 says, "'Because the poor are plundered, because the needy groan, I will now arise,' says the LORD; 'I will place him in the safety for which he longs'" (ESV). God is squarely opposed to the abuse you've experienced, and He is rising up on your behalf to bring you both justice and freedom as He delivers you to the safe haven of His love.

As your parched soul drinks from the life-giving Scriptures contained in this devotional, my prayer is that you will experience deliverance—in every way possible—as your rescue story unfolds. God knows you long for a safe haven; in the weariness and brokenness, He promises to be the place you can finally call home.

NOTES ABOUT THIS DEVOTIONAL

This book features twenty-one devotional entries divided into three sections. Each of these sections addresses a different component of the abuse recovery experience:

1) The Hurt
2) The Hiding Place
3) The Healing

While each of these facets is addressed individually, experience has shown me that God often works on these things in a more simultaneous fashion. Healing is not a linear process, and often God will guide us through a layered approach, revisiting areas we thought we'd dealt with to ensure our recovery and restoration are thorough and complete. Due to the depth and breadth of abuse experiences, I'm certain I've not addressed every possible angle of this topic, nor will everything I have included pertain to your specific recovery journey. For those limitations, I petition your grace. Some of what I've written will cut straight to the core and may prompt some strong emotional responses. Other parts may not resonate, but I pray they might offer you a glimpse into the diverse experiences we in this courageous community must endure. Either way, I invite you into the beauty that is curiosity as you consider new vantages and viewpoints. I pray that what you will find here will ignite a flame of hope along your journey and leave you with the sense that you are so completely loved and never alone.

Writing this book has been an emotionally arduous journey for me, but it has been a profound mile marker on my own road of restoration as well. Thank you for being a part of it.

NOTE: You may notice in this book that I often refer to a person who has been abused as a "target" or "victim." I must be clear that these words are not labels—they do *not* define you or identify you as a person. They are only used here to describe the experience of a person who has been abused within an abusive relationship dynamic.

Also, while this devotional addresses the spiritual implications of abuse, there are emotional, mental, and physical needs that I also encourage you to tend to through professional, individual counseling. As we'll touch on later, couple and family counseling with the abuser is not appropriate or recommended. Before confronting or separating from an abuser, or if you feel you are in danger, please seek guidance from a domestic violence shelter, hotline professional, or counselor who is a domestic violence specialist.

SECTION 1

The Hurt

Jesus answered them,
"It is not the healthy who need
a doctor, but the sick."

LUKE 5:31

Several years ago, my mom developed some troubling physical symptoms. It started out as trouble swallowing, and after a frightening choking incident, she consulted a gastrointestinal specialist. The doctor assessed my mother's entire array of symptoms, which included some additional muscular weakness, and sensed that the issue was neuromuscular. My mom was referred to a neurologist.

After a short consultation, the neurologist ordered a battery of painful tests for my mother to endure—like stick-needles-in-your-body-and-shock-you-senseless kind of painful. The results were inconclusive. The doctor, one of the premiere specialists in the region, was absolutely stumped. Not a good sign.

With each passing week, my mom became weaker and more desperate for answers. The physician suggested perhaps the problem was an autoimmune condition known as polymyositis, in which the inflammation of muscle tissues causes weakening throughout the body. The conventional treatment for that disease requires heavy doses of steroids, which my mother began right away.

Despite the treatment, my mother's condition worsened. Within three months, she could no longer walk or lift herself out of a chair. The steroids had several uncomfortable side effects, including significant and painful swelling all over her body. Within a few months, my active, fifty-five-year-old mother appeared to all of us to be standing at death's doorstep.

We returned to the neurologist. He questioned his diagnosis. It was clear the steroids were killing my mom. He said to her, "I hope I didn't do this to you." Not exactly what we wanted to hear.

In a last-ditch effort, my mother applied to be seen at the Mayo Clinic in Scottsdale, Arizona. After being approved, she met with a team of specialists who diagnosed her with a rare autoimmune condition known as necrotizing autoimmune myopathy—a condition in which the body attacks and destroys its own muscle tissue. The steroids she had been taking were doubling the damage. They abruptly stopped her medication, and she began a regimen of immune-suppressing drugs proven to be effective for her newly diagnosed condition. Within weeks she began to regain her strength, and I'm so pleased to say that while she did suffer some irreversible muscle damage, she's resumed her duties as a highly active grandmother of three (and avid chicken farmer).

Looking back, the reason my mom experienced such a delay in receiving the help she desperately needed was that the neurologist had started in the wrong place, with the wrong diagnosis. However, the Mayo specialists' correct conclusions allowed her to receive the proper care, and her deteriorating condition was quickly reversed.

THE WRONG DIAGNOSIS

So often, individuals who are suffering abuse know something is wrong, but they can't pin down exactly what's going on. You may know the person who has been hurting you is argumentative; addicted to drugs, alcohol, or sex; critical; jealous; reckless; deceitful; dismissive; and likely more. But the reason the hurt is so hard to see is that this person also presents themselves as charming, concerned, adoring, impressive, apologetic, or generous. The experience of being abused is absolutely disorienting. Love and pain mixed together can make a dangerous and confusing cocktail. As a result of this fog of confusion, those who are being abused are just not able to properly diagnose and treat the situation themselves.

There are all kinds of remedies for "troubled relationships," and perhaps you've tried a few. Counseling, therapeutic intensives, retreats, interventions, Bible studies, recovery groups—the options are many. You may have even felt that you've witnessed a little progress, but eventually things tend to end up back where they started. I'm sure at one time or another you've caught yourself wondering, *Why doesn't anything work?*

To quote one of my all-time favorite movies, *Indiana Jones and the Raiders of the Lost Ark*, "They're digging in the wrong place."[1]

The problem is, you cannot apply a remedy for a "troubled relationship" to an abusive relationship. These are different diagnoses with different treatments. It's not wrong to start with treatments for strained relationships, but when they don't work, we must be willing to shift the diagnosis and try different tactics.

Many people are not aware that the Bible offers us different solutions to our relational problems. Most often the confusion stems from the multitude of teachings from the Bible about being longsuffering and patient when it comes to those in need of grace and, likewise, loving our enemies. It is often suggested that abuse victims should "turn the other cheek," with the hope that the other person will soften their heart and turn to Jesus, because "love covers a multitude of sins" (Matthew 5:39; 1 Peter 4:8, author's paraphrase).

Don't get me wrong—these things are absolutely true in their given applications. But "turn the other cheek" in context could be better understood as "don't retaliate." Is that really how it's used when talking to those in abuse situations? No. Instead, it's been used to coax abuse victims into silently suffering abuse. Verses such as these are often cherry-picked and removed from their context, then misapplied in ways that the Bible did not intend (which is damaging at best and spiritual abuse at worst). Thankfully, for people dealing with abusive relationship dynamics, the Bible has a whole lot more to say on the subject and goes far beyond a simplistic grin-and-bear-it theology.

I was stuck for a long time too—for the better part of two decades. But once I could put a name to my situation, I began to see things I'd previously missed, and I began gaining a strength I didn't know I could have. My desire for you is that you begin this recovery journey with the right diagnosis for the hurt you've experienced so you'll have eyes to see the truth of your circumstances and the potential of what awaits you on the other side.

WHAT IS ABUSE EXACTLY?

Simply put, abuse is any pattern or combination of behaviors one person uses to establish power over and control of another, especially when it comes to that person's ability to enjoy and exercise their God-given individuality and free will.

There are several categories of abuse, and abusive individuals often use more than one type of abuse in their efforts to dominate their targets. These types include (but are not limited to) the following:

- **Physical Abuse:** Inflicting physical harm or intimidating a person using any physical or bodily means, such as slapping, biting, kicking, punching, grabbing, hair-pulling, throwing/damaging objects, etc. Also includes restraining or following a person, neglecting someone's physical needs, preventing sleep, controlling food intake, forcing the use of substances, physically abandoning someone, or prohibiting someone from seeking medical/personal care.

- **Verbal or Emotional Abuse:** Taunting, harassing, name-calling, threatening, lying or withholding the truth, manipulating, frequently "forgetting," blaming, shaming, body shaming, minimizing or denying, gaslighting, making someone feel crazy, cursing, giving the silent treatment, and spreading false information. Often also involves social isolation and using one's personal relationships as leverage (including children and pets). Also includes apologizing without sustained change and rejecting or abandoning someone's emotional needs.
- **Sexual Abuse:** Exploiting another person for personal sexual gratification, sexual threats, or the withholding of sexual intimacy as punishment. Also includes non-consensual sexual acts as well as sexual coercion, rape, molestation, porn usage, and unwanted comments that are sexual in nature.
- **Spiritual Abuse:** Using spirituality, Scriptures, or church standing to establish one's own dominance by manipulating, shaming, or coercing others. Might also use similar means to justify or excuse improper

conduct. Also includes harassing and ridiculing a person's beliefs, preventing someone from practicing their faith, using church relationships and leadership against a person, and forcing someone to act against their conscience.

- **Financial or Resource Abuse:** Withholding or restricting financial resources and financial information (sometimes disguised as an "allowance" for a spouse), reckless spending, frequent requests for money, intentional and chronic joblessness, stealing, and fraud (credit, tax, etc.).

Reading through this list, you may have been caught off guard by the fact that certain behaviors you thought were normal for your situation are actually abusive. This may have also brought up some hard feelings for you. If so, take a pause right now and grieve what has been done to you. Pauses are good and necessary for inviting God's healing into those spaces where we have been wounded.

You also may find yourself wondering, *How did I miss this?* Due to the covert, hidden nature of abuse, those who are being abused are often not aware of it until it is revealed by a third party. That's why questions like "Why didn't you leave?" and "Why didn't you speak up?" aren't helpful. Chances are, the level of deception is so great that a victim is lacking the necessary information to put all the pieces together. After all, the whole point of deception is that you never realize you're being deceived.

But not knowing you've been abused doesn't mean you are stupid or oblivious. To most of us, it is unfathomable that someone would hurt us *on purpose*. Read that again: abuse is always *on purpose*. Abusers have developed a worldview that sees relationships and people as things to exploit, and they *intentionally* manipulate, avoid, hide, or explain away circumstances to maintain control, keeping you unaware and off balance.

And yes, they know what they are doing.

You might also be reading this list and thinking, *But I've done some of these things. Am I the abuser?* Despite the "shrinking violet" depiction of the abuse victim, it's not uncommon for someone who is being abused to react strongly to the mistreatment they're receiving. The mental and emotional toll of relational abuse is hauntingly similar to that of the torture inflicted upon prisoners of war.[2] But reacting to abuse does not make you an abuser. Nor does it mean that you are to blame for the abuse. Remember, abuse involves an *intent* to misuse and control someone, and a reaction does not involve that same intent.

As we'll uncover in more detail, true abusers are intentionally opportunistic and constantly on the offense (as Peter describes Satan in 1 Peter 5:8, someone who "prowls around"). They use excruciating methods to instigate problems—on purpose.[3] This ensures you'll either fold up entirely and surrender to their demands or be pushed to the point of emotional collapse. If that happens, the abuser gains the upper hand by shaming you for your reactions, shifting the focus (and the blame) off them and onto you. But this in itself is another control tactic.

Reacting to abuse keeps you trapped underneath its power. Your reactions are currency in the economy of abuse—they are a sure sign to the abuser that they still have influence in your life.

Because your reactions may be a tether to this toxic economy, denying the abuser your reaction is a powerful way to break loose of the bondage of abuse.

I am not saying not to have feelings—what you are experiencing is valid and real. But rather than *reacting* to the abuse, your emotions and logic can work together to instead propel you to meaningfully *respond* to the situation (which can actually mean offering no response at all).

The goal in healing from the hurt of abuse is to restore your dignity and identity as a separate and unique image bearer of God. But before we start down that road, you must first know that you have an identity and image worth fighting for, worth dying for. Psalm 72:12–14 says: "For he will deliver the needy who cry out, the afflicted who have no one to help. He will take pity on the weak and the needy and save the needy from death. He will rescue them from oppression and violence, for precious is their blood in his sight."

God Himself is for you. He is not ashamed of you. He is not embarrassed by you, and He certainly hasn't forgotten you. His heart is to lift you out of shame and lead you out of oppression. And while the process of deliverance can bring soul-wrenching grief, it also brings tremendous freedom as God guides you away from the hurt and into His safe haven.

GOD HATES ABUSE

> There are six things the LORD hates, seven that are detestable to him: haughty eyes, a lying tongue, hands that shed innocent blood, a heart that devises wicked schemes, feet that are quick to rush into evil, a false witness who pours out lies and a person who stirs up conflict in the community.
> **PROVERBS 6:16–19**

I can comfortably say that the average Christian isn't exactly sure what God even thinks about abuse. Before my healing journey began, I certainly wasn't. With so many verses about loving our enemies and forgiveness, we can deduce that we are supposed to turn a blind eye when people mistreat us. But when you're being abused, something about that also seems completely off, like we're just offering them the opportunity to hurt us again.

The Bible clearly indicates that God hates the arrogant, deceitful, predatory, ruinous, and divisive nature of abusive people (see Proverbs 6:16–19 above). And if we look closely, this passage doesn't merely say that God detests the *actions* and *behaviors* of abusive individuals. He abhors *the person*.

This passage describes the individual characteristics of an abuser's character—haughty, lying, wicked, false—all represented by parts of the body. But these parts are not separate, nor do they act alone. These parts form and reveal the whole of the person, a person set against God at his or her core.

When we pull all this together, we see that in God's eyes, abuse is not simply actions. It's not even just a bad attitude or a selfish mindset. It's an indication of someone who is spiritually darkened with a heart set against God.

We can see this spiritual reality further echoed in Titus 3:10–11, in which Paul writes, "Warn a divisive person once, and then warn them a second time. After that, have nothing to do with them. You may be sure that such people are warped and sinful; they are self-condemned." Paul writes similarly in 2 Timothy 3:8, "They are men of depraved minds, who, as far as the faith is concerned, are rejected."

Warped. Self-condemned. Rejected.

The methods abusers use to control and manipulate might vary, but there's still a common thread: their actions are born of a deeply rebellious spirit. And out of a sin-sickened spirit comes wicked thoughts that give way to destructive actions.

Accepting this truth is not always as easy as we think it should be. At first, you may experience a measure of comfort knowing that God opposes your abuser. You may feel some relief as you sense that God not only sees your suffering but that He's disgusted by it, in all His holy fury. But that relief often yields to shame over the things you've gotten wrong in this life too, as well as the horror of realizing someone you have loved may be an enemy of God. It's a frightful thing. But for right now, in the swirl of tangled emotions, I want to settle you back under the protection of God's love and His righteous anger over what you've had to endure. In time, we will unravel the rest.

Notice, in this moment, if you've ever found yourself minimizing, discounting, or excusing the mistreatment you've suffered. Recognize the thought patterns that resist the notion that the person who has hurt you is spiritually opposed to God. Perhaps the person who wounded you had a traumatic childhood, and you've understood their hurtful behaviors as reaction to that. Or perhaps you've believed they just don't manage stress well or were born with a short fuse. Maybe you believe that you are no different or no better.

Pay attention to these thoughts at the outset of your healing journey. Observe how they might shift and change as you go. Abuse distorts our view of reality so deftly that we believe there must be a reasonable explanation for it (other than just plain old evil). But such justifications are precisely what keep you close when you should get to safety.

God doesn't minimize your abuse; He flat-out hates it. Part of the process of recovering from abuse is learning to retrain our minds to see things as God sees them, and His Word guides us in doing just that. Since God's Word describes abuse as wicked, you are invited to describe it as wicked. It says God hates abuse, so you can now learn to hate it. And when it says He's angry about how you've been treated, you can know that it is right to be angry about how you've been treated. Understanding God's attitude toward abuse empowers you to respond to it as He does and ushers order and light into places of confusion and darkness.

Reflection and Prayer

Where has your view of abuse not aligned with God's view? How does adjusting your understanding of abuse change the way you think God sees you? How would you like to change the way you relate to Him?

In your time of prayer, consider asking God to guide you in assessing your circumstances through the lens of His Word. Ask Him to reveal what you need to see, and ask Him to comfort and strengthen you by His Spirit as the truth is unveiled.

JESUS KNOWS

> We do not have a high priest who is unable to empathize with our weaknesses, but we have one who has been tempted in every way, just as we are—yet he did not sin. Let us then approach God's throne of grace with confidence, so that we may receive mercy and find grace to help us in our time of need.
> **HEBREWS 4:15–16**

I'm often asked if there are stories of abuse in the Bible—if there is evidence of the kind of wicked exploitation and oppression we've been talking about.

My response? "Get a pen."

There are several pointed accounts of malicious abusers in the Bible; one of the most detailed is the story of King Saul in the Old Testament. The book of 1 Samuel describes Saul as a man with a fierce devotion to his own glory, without much fervor for the glory of God (1 Samuel 13–15). On more than one occasion, Saul arrogantly rebelled against God's commands. He had an established pattern of rashly disobeying God's instructions, then begging for forgiveness, only to return to his wicked ways again and again.

Saul was also known for denying and twisting the truth. As Samuel scolded Saul for an instance of disobedience, Saul retorted,

"But I did obey the Lord" (1 Samuel 15:20). This was a half-truth—but a half-truth is still a full lie. Saul then went on to justify his behavior as he listed his many accomplishments as the ruler of God's people. But Samuel wasn't fooled. He pointed out Saul's attempts to veil the truth and stated that due to Saul's repeated offenses, God had finally rejected him as king. Saul then pathetically excused his disobedience by shifting the blame to the Israelites, saying he "was afraid of the men" and "gave in to them" (v. 24).

As if this wasn't enough, Saul committed many other abusive acts. In multiple fits of rage, Saul physically assaulted David. Saul plotted to have David murdered and even exploited his own daughter in the process, using her as bait (1 Samuel 18). Saul was exceedingly jealous of David and repeatedly manipulated David's esteem for him, concealing his true intentions to take David down.

The Bible also describes the toxic pairing of King Ahab and Queen Jezebel. Quite the entitled couple, both used their positions to lord over their subjects and take advantage of them. First Kings 21 describes King Ahab's failed attempt to goad a man into a negotiation in which Ahab would acquire (and then decimate) the man's vineyard. Talk about an abuse of power. Ahab was the king! Ahab returned home sulking and rejected, but the scheming Jezebel jumped into action. She usurped Ahab's power, forging letters in his name to falsely accuse the landowner, and ordered the man executed. She instructed Ahab to return to the vineyard and take possession of it, free of charge (and he willingly obliged, of course). Like Saul, Ahab was also known for repeated, unremorseful apologies, and Jezebel is described as vain and sharp-tongued, vicious in her dealings with the prophet Elijah.

First Samuel 25 also gives the account of another abusive man by the name of Nabal, the wicked husband of a woman named Abigail. In this passage, Nabal is described as a wealthy man, "surly and mean in his dealings" (v. 3). A servant described Nabal as "such a wicked man that no one can talk to him" (v. 17). In his travels, the not-yet-king David and his men encountered Nabal's shepherds in the wilderness and acted kindly toward them. David sent messengers to bring greetings and make a friendly request for provisions during the festival season in return for his kindness. In his greed, Nabal rejected David's request, cutting him down with a verbal attack of insults in the process. In his pride, Nabal endangered his wife and servants as the furious David and his armed men threatened an attack on the entire household.

And then there's Judas. Like these other unsavory characters, Judas was also known for masking his true motives and for his greed. John 12 tells of a woman who anointed Jesus' feet with a bottle of expensive perfume. Shocked by the scene, Judas said, "Why wasn't this perfume sold and the money given to the poor?" (v. 5). But gospel writer John further revealed Judas's underlying intentions, saying, "He did not say this because he cared about the poor but because he was a thief; as keeper of the money bag, he used to help himself to what was put into it" (v. 6).

Judas used his special position as one of the twelve disciples to get close to Jesus, plot against Him, and then betray Him—all for his own selfish gain. Not only did Judas acquire wealth in the process of abusing Jesus, but he also received esteem from the religious leaders who conspired with him. He was a man of ulterior motives, and he was willing to sell out the Son of God in pursuit of his own glory.

While these villains each terrorized their targets with a uniquely horrendous combination of abusive behaviors, a thread of hope is woven through each of these stories. In every single one of these instances, God made a way for the targeted victim to be rescued.

David was able to flee from Saul until Saul was wounded in battle and eventually committed suicide. David also found favor with God, was appointed king, and received an honored position in both Jewish history and the genealogy of Jesus. Elijah escaped from Ahab and Jezebel (who were both executed) and was taken up into heaven without ever experiencing natural death. Abigail was able to convince David not to destroy Nabal's household. When Nabal suddenly died of a presumed stroke, David took Abigail as his wife. In each of these stories, God brought liberation to the abused, and He further blessed them with His care and loving-kindness.

As for Jesus, He had to stay close to Judas for the means of our salvation and eternal rescue from sin. But through the ordeal, and its rendering in Scripture, Jesus also offers us a hope we can cling to in this life, knowing that in our abuse we have the compassion of a Savior who suffered in the same way. Jesus knows.

Reflection and Prayer

What feelings come up for you when you hear that God desires rescue and blessing for the abused? Recognizing that Jesus suffered as you have, how do you understand His relationship to you differently?

In your time of prayer, consider sitting with God and soaking in His love and compassion for you. Ask Him to reveal His thoughts toward you and what He longs to rescue you from and for.

THE GASLIGHTING OF EVE

> "You belong to your father, the devil, and you want to carry out your father's desires. He was a murderer from the beginning, not holding to the truth, for there is no truth in him. When he lies, he speaks his native language, for he is a liar and the father of lies."
> **JOHN 8:44**

Jesus spoke these words to a group of unbelieving Jews and Pharisees, describing the characteristics of Satan as a liar and deceiver. In this passage, Jesus wants the hearers to know the enemy has been spinning a web of lies from the beginning. In fact, if we go back to Genesis, we can actually study the first account of abuse in the Bible.

In the Garden of Eden, the enemy approached Eve in the form of a serpent and engaged in a form of abuse known as gaslighting. Gaslighting is a subtle yet extremely damaging form of control in which the perpetrator destabilizes their victim by openly denying or casting doubt on the reality of a situation. Gaslighting takes many forms, but some obvious examples include saying "I didn't say that" about something they definitely said, or suggesting "You don't know what you're talking about" when you bring up a concern. An abuser who is gaslighting may also change the facts of a story to present an alternate narrative around what happened, creating confusion for the victim. Gaslighting is often subtle, yet it is methodical, and it slowly erodes the victim's sense of self and ability to perceive reality over time. It's one of the major reasons someone in a relationship would say, "I feel like I'm going crazy."

Now back to the gaslighting of Eve. The enemy made his approach in Genesis 3:1, saying to Eve, "Did God really say, 'You must not eat from any tree in the garden'?"

At the outset, Eve knew this was obviously false. She knew it wasn't *any* tree but one specific tree they were instructed not to touch. She responded in verses 2–3, "We may eat fruit from the trees in the garden, but God did say, 'You must not eat fruit from the tree that is in the middle of the garden, and you must not touch it, or you will die.'"

What Eve was not aware of during this pithy dialogue was the fact that the enemy had subtly created a connection with her in an attempt to disarm her. Rather than go straight for the kill at the beginning, the enemy chose to draw Eve toward him first, with what appeared to be mere conversation. Not only that, but he began the dialogue in a way that actually built up her confidence—he gave her the opportunity to show off her knowledge in correcting his blatant error in mentioning "any tree." He knew it was not *any* tree. But he wanted Eve to believe that he was harmless and that she might have had the upper hand. Such charming behavior is often seen with abusers; victims may initially experience a period of time when they feel valued, loved, favored, or chosen.

After Eve's defenses were lowered, the enemy upped the ante and slyly went on the offensive. In verses 4–5 he continued, suggesting, "You will not certainly die . . . For God knows that when you eat from it your eyes will be opened, and you will be like God, knowing good and evil."

While Eve's guard was down, the enemy assaulted her with a counterfeit reality, causing her to question the truth. He in effect said to her, "You don't know what you're talking about." I can imagine the questions that must have swirled around Eve in this moment: *Why not this tree? Why wouldn't God want me to be like Him? Would He really do that? Doesn't He love me? Is there something wrong with me?*

What is so exceedingly detrimental about the enemy's deception of Eve is that the doubt he deposited in her mind was about so much more than just fruit. Eve became uncertain of her entire reality: God, herself, and the world around her. Abuse victims often experience a similar fog of confusion. In Eve's case, the doubt she experienced created so much internal chaos that she ended up siding with her abuser, rejecting the truth she had proclaimed with her own mouth just moments before.

Like many of us, Eve never saw it coming.

One of the hallmarks of abuse is that it creates extreme confusion in the person targeted, along with self-doubt, self-blame, shame, and fear of the outside world. Gaslighting is designed to strip a victim of their individuality and independence, often causing them to look to the abuser for stability. It's in this vulnerable state that the abuser may isolate the victim (whether physically or socially) and possibly coerce the victim to do things they might not otherwise do. All the while, the victim is completely unaware of what's happening—that it's the abuser who is actually pulling the strings.

On top of that, alternating between love and hate creates a sense of utter internal chaos. To make sense of the madness, victims usually end up convincing themselves that what's happening is partially their fault. We say things like "If only I were a better _____" or "They wouldn't do that if I didn't do _____." But that's the shame talking. Gaslighting causes the target to believe something is inherently wrong with them, which may have been Eve's experience.

But when we know that abuse distorts our view of reality, we can start taking steps to get out from beneath the lies we've believed and discover what it's like to walk in the light of truth. First Corinthians 14:33 says, "God is not a God of confusion but of peace" (ESV). God desires unparalleled peace for His people, and that includes peace in our minds, emotions, and relationships. Lies cause confusion, but when we seek to be blanketed by truth, we can experience greater degrees of peace, freedom, and restoration.

Reflection and Prayer

Have you felt confused or destabilized by gaslighting? What lies or distortions have caused you to be plagued by doubt and shame? How has that doubt affected your view of God, yourself, and your choices? What new beliefs do you need to integrate in order to stamp out the lies?

In your prayer time, consider asking God to help you gain clarity and peace by uprooting confusion. Ask Him to guide you in discernment to uncover life-giving truth. Sit with Him in stillness and allow yourself to experience His love and peace washing over you.

4

SEPARATING FROM THE SOURCE

> Mark this: There will be terrible times in the last days. People will be lovers of themselves, lovers of money, boastful, proud, abusive, disobedient to their parents, ungrateful, unholy, without love, unforgiving, slanderous, without self-control, brutal, not lovers of the good, treacherous, rash, conceited, lovers of pleasure rather than lovers of God—having a form of godliness but denying its power. Have nothing to do with such people.
>
> **2 TIMOTHY 3:1–5**

Of any passage on abuse in the Bible, 2 Timothy 3:1–5 is one of the clearest in not only describing abuse but also explaining what to do about it. In it, Paul lays out for Timothy the hallmark behaviors of toxic individuals. Timothy was rising up to take Paul's place, and before he died, Paul wanted Timothy to know that not everyone he encountered in his ministry would have pure motives. Paul made it especially clear that this included what we would think of as "church people." Paul knew that churches were, and still are, one of the best places for predatory abusers to build stellar reputations while grooming vulnerable targets.

Paul knew such exploitive people would threaten the physical, emotional, and spiritual safety of our homes and communities. Because of that fact, Paul did not merely suggest that Timothy separate himself from such people; he commanded it.

And Paul was not the only one to give this guidance. Jesus laid out an entire process for separating from unrepentant sinners (including abusers) in Matthew 18. In verses 15–17, He said:

> "If your brother or sister sins, go and point out their fault, just between the two of you. If they listen to you, you have won them over. But if they will not listen, take one or two others along, so that 'every matter may be established by the testimony of two or three witnesses.' If they still refuse to listen, tell it to the church; and if they refuse to listen even to the church, treat them as you would a pagan or a tax collector."

Jesus knew that we would encounter spiritually darkened people in our lives and that we'd need a way to confront them. In Jesus' process, such a person is given multiple opportunities to turn things around before the consequences of separation kick in. We can observe their behavior to gauge the condition of a person's spiritual health (or lack thereof). While this process gives the person in the wrong multiple opportunities to change, it also gives you multiple opportunities to determine the content of their character. Do they really think they are wrong, or do they make excuses and blame others? Are they taking steps to change on their own, or do they give up after a handful of attempts?

Jesus tells us to truly discern the answers to these questions; we can't settle for mere apologies, half-hearted attempts to change, and grand displays of emotion. Abusers will use such tactics to avoid accountability. Rather, to know a tree by its fruit (Matthew 7:15–20), we have to consider a person's actions when confronted with the reality of their behavior. If after multiple warnings the sinful patterns don't change, Jesus says we have all the evidence we need to consider them as "a pagan or a tax collector"—in other words, an unbeliever.

Why does categorizing this person as an "unbeliever" matter anyway? If someone is proclaiming to be a follower of God yet behaves in ways contrary to that claim, Jesus cautions us to change the nature of the relationship with this person based on what they *do* rather than simply believing what they *say*. Why? It all comes down to trust.

You cannot have a relationship with a person you cannot trust. A person who lacks consistency between words and deeds also lacks consistency in their character and isn't to be trusted with your spiritual, emotional, and physical well-being. In our closest relationships, we are extremely vulnerable, and the people we engage with have the power to hurt us or heal us in critical ways. It's in relationships where we expose our deepest pains and brokenness to those who pledge to love us. But someone who routinely shows love for themselves over love for others does not have God's love abiding in them and is a danger to us in our vulnerability. For our protection, we're not called to "stick it out." We're called to create emotional, spiritual, and physical space.

A quick note here: you'll notice that when the Bible talks about separating from a wicked person, nowhere does it say, "except if you're married," or "except if you're dealing with a parent." This guidance is for all of us, in every type of relationship. As you consider Jesus' guidance from Matthew 18, make sure that you're surrounded by a council of trustworthy Christ followers, committed to discerning and upholding truth. Should you find the process corrupted or those involved untrustworthy or uncommitted to your safety, seek additional support.

One of the reasons it is essential to separate and get to safety when dealing with an abusive person is that abusers thrive off their ability to get a reaction (whether positive or negative). A reaction lets an abuser know he or she has influence and the power to manipulate another person at will. You get mad, they win. They lie and get away with it, they win. You give them another chance when they apologize, they win. They convince a therapist you're the crazy one, they win (which is why marriage or family counseling is not recommended in cases of abuse). Just as alcoholics are addicted to using alcohol, abusers are addicted to using people.

Sometimes your mere presence is enough to keep them coming back for more, and you have to remove yourself if they are ever going to stop focusing on you long enough to examine themselves and turn from their sin. It's why Paul said in 1 Corinthians 5:5 to "hand this man over to Satan for the destruction of the flesh, so that his spirit may be saved on the day of the Lord." You do not separate with the intention to shame or condemn the person, but you do it to preserve your safety while allowing them to experience consequences that may cause them to fully repent and experience salvation, should they choose that path.

You should know that separating can be the most dangerous time for an abuse victim, even if no physical violence took place before the separation. Sometimes it's more prudent to quietly distance yourself from an abuser rather than making an official declaration. Proverbs 9:7 says, "Whoever corrects a mocker invites insults; whoever rebukes the wicked incurs abuse." Abusers are often not capable of healthy communication, so announcing your intention to create some distance between you may open the door to angry threats and retaliation. Before you take action to separate from an abusive person, contact a domestic violence counselor or hotline to develop a safety plan. Quietly get yourself to safety first, then deal with how to communicate your boundaries after that.

The biggest takeaway here is that if nothing changes, nothing changes. Ephesians 5:11 says, "Have nothing to do with the fruitless deeds of darkness, but rather expose them." If in exposing darkness the abuser decides not to change anything, the tragic and unfair reality is that the target of abuse often has to be the one to change things instead. But Jesus and Paul both knew this would likely be so, and thankfully they illuminated the way.

Unfortunately, even when you create distance with an abuser, they may not choose to repent. They may simply move on to another source of emotional supply. But regardless of what they choose, the time and space apart give you the clarity to see the full picture, the opportunity to heal, and the freedom to become who God has made you to be.

Reflection and Prayer

Have you been reluctant to distance yourself from an abusive person? How has your perspective shifted? What is your next step to securing safety for yourself—physically, mentally, emotionally, or spiritually?

In your time of prayer, consider asking God to show you how to start creating distance with an individual (or individuals) who are hurting you. Ask Him to provide you with wise people who can help you create a safety plan.

5

CAN THEY CHANGE?

The fear of the Lord is the beginning of knowledge, but fools despise wisdom and instruction.
PROVERBS 1:7

Wisdom and respect for God go hand in hand: the greater our desire to honor God and His ways, the wiser we become. But this whole equation works the other way around too: the more a person rejects God and His instructions, the more hard-hearted and foolish they become.

The book of Proverbs describes foolishness as a spectrum, using six different words to reveal the state of a person's heart. It covers everything from simpleminded naivety all the way down to hardened wickedness. To understand the nature of abusers, it's important to look at the differences along this spectrum.

Let's start with what the book of Proverbs calls "the simple," marked by the Hebrew word *pthiy*. The simple are not particularly wise or especially foolish, but they are given to moments of each. The simple can best be understood as gullible, immature, or naive (Proverbs 14:15). When really lacking in judgment, the simple may be drawn toward pleasure without considering the cause-and-effect consequences of their actions (Proverbs 7). We've all been in the seat of the simple, and in certain areas of our lives we may still be there. The good news is that while the simple can be open-minded about all kinds of wrong ideas, Scripture says they are also still open-minded toward God's instruction.

But when someone who is spiritually simple does not grow in the Lord, we begin to see the characteristics of "the fool," or in Hebrew, the word *kesil*. The fool hates wisdom and instruction (Proverbs 1:22) and does not feel guilty about their wrongdoing (14:9). The fool is hot-tempered (27:3), unforgiving (14:9), reckless (14:16), mischievous (10:23), and self-destructive (1:32). Some of the bullies and other toxic people we encounter in our lives would be best understood as fools.

We may be tempted to "help" a fool or talk to them about their behavior and attitudes. But trying to change a fool is futile and more likely to wear us out in the process; Proverbs 27:22 says, "You cannot separate fools from their foolishness, even though you grind them like grain with mortar and pestle" (NLT). Worse yet, the fool is dangerous; not only is a fool headed for personal disaster, but one of their defining traits is that they bring others down with them. Proverbs 13:20 says that "a companion of fools suffers harm," and Proverbs 26:4 cautions us to stay away from foolish people because it's very likely we'll become foolish ourselves.

Like the simple, the foolish may still have soft enough hearts to respond to the instruction of the Lord. Proverbs 8:5 says, "You who are simple, gain prudence; you who are foolish, set your hearts on it." God offers wisdom to those who would choose to allow their lives to be changed by it. But when it comes to relating to the foolish, we are cautioned to remove ourselves from the process and allow God to do the work (which is exactly what we talked about in relation to the separation process in Matthew 18).

If the heart of a fool continues to harden against God, a person may be consumed by absolute wickedness. Proverbs describes this person as "the mocker" or "a scoffer," denoted in Hebrew by the words *luts*, *nabal*, and *rasha*. Remember Nabal from the story of David and Abigail? This is where his name came from. A mocker is arrogant and self-indulgent (Proverbs 21:24) and takes delight in being condemning and critical (1:22). The mocker constantly manipulates people and situations for selfish gain (24:9), trusts in their own power (11:7), and puts on a front to create a false impression (21:29). The mocker not only has no remorse for their sin, but they scoff at the very thought that they've even done anything wrong (14:9). They are ruthless and uncooperative, and they have a lust for all things sensuous and self-gratifying.

When it comes to this kind of wickedness, the Bible implies that the person we're dealing with is guilty of significant willful rebellion against God (again, regardless of whether they claim to be a believer). They are so entrenched in evil that they can't even see it or perceive it anymore. Proverbs 4:19 says that "the way of the wicked is like deep darkness; they do not know what makes them stumble." That's one of the reasons pointing it out is, well, pointless.

Fools suffer consequences for their choices, but mockers have offended God to the extent that they can expect His wrath. Proverbs 19:29 says that "judgments are prepared for mockers, and beatings for the backs of fools" (BSB).

And that's why Proverbs 22:10 says to get far away from a mocker. When we do, "out goes strife" and "quarrels and insults are ended."

Jesus summed this all up in His parable of the weeds in Matthew 13. He described a sower who sowed good seed into a field, only to have his enemy sow weeds in the field behind him. After sharing the parable, Jesus explained in verses 37–43:

> "The one who sowed the good seed is the Son of Man. The field is the world, and the good seed stands for the people of the kingdom. The weeds are the people of the evil one, and the enemy who sows them is the devil. The harvest is the end of the age, and the harvesters are angels.
>
> "As the weeds are pulled up and burned in the fire, so it will be at the end of the age. The Son of Man will send out his angels, and they will weed out of his kingdom everything that causes sin and all who do evil. They will throw them into the blazing furnace, where there will be weeping and gnashing of teeth. Then the righteous will shine like the sun in the kingdom of their Father. Whoever has ears, let them hear."

I'm not a green thumb, but in studying this parable, I learned that young wheat plants in this region of the Middle East appear to be nearly identical to the young weed plants; it's not always easy to distinguish which is which just by looking at them in their immature state. But as these plants grow, the differences become glaringly obvious; the wheat plants grow taller and develop thicker stalks than the weed plants. Over time and with careful observation, the truth is much clearer.

The same is true with the people we encounter in our lives. At the outset, it can be difficult to figure out if a person just has some bad habits or if they're developing a hardened heart. The differences become more obvious as we all spiritually mature (or don't), but it's something that the Bible tells us to gauge from a safe distance when possible.

And while you may not be certain if the person who has hurt you can change, that's a process that you just can't be a part of—for your benefit and for theirs. If you stay involved, it's like prey trying to help a predator. It just doesn't work. What you need to know is that there is still hope for your future. You were created on purpose for a purpose. It's that purpose that God releases you to as your eyes are opened and you begin to break free from the grip of wickedness.

Reflection and Prayer

How does reflecting on the difference between wisdom and wickedness help you understand the mistreatment you've endured? Do you need to release yourself from concerns about whether the person who has hurt you can change?

In your prayer time, consider seeking God's protection over your heart and mind. Ask to grow in wisdom and discernment and for the comfort and confidence to make adjustments to your relationships where needed.

6

IT'S NOT YOUR FAULT

Godly sorrow brings repentance that leads to salvation and leaves no regret, but worldly sorrow brings death.
2 CORINTHIANS 7:10

In healthy adult relationships, there should be a balance of giving and receiving. Both people involved in a pairing (whether romantic, platonic, or familial) should expect to experience both the sacrifice of giving and the blessing of receiving in complementary amounts.

Many somewhat normal relationships flounder when the balance of giving and receiving is out of whack. It's healthy for both parties to take a good look at themselves to figure out what they're contributing (or not contributing) to the problem. But because of this approach in typical relationships, many people wrongly assume that the same sort of imbalance is what causes abusive dynamics—that a victim must be doing something that causes the abuser to lash out. This is called victim blaming, and while it seems logical, it doesn't apply to a situation in which an abuser is intentionally seeking to dominate or manipulate the other person.

The truth is, abuse does not have a cause-and-effect nature. You cannot cause someone to choose to abuse you. There are dozens of ways to handle legitimate concerns in relationships that are not abusive, but abuse is *not* a relationship problem between two people. Rather, the abuser's individual heart problem has led them to an unhealthy perspective on relationships, revealed in their inappropriate choices.

Your abuse is not your fault.

Abuse thrives on a lopsided equation in which the abuser consistently consumes far more than they contribute. As we looked at previously, greed is a sure sign of someone who is foolish or wicked. To understand the madness of abuse, we have to correct our understanding of the way abusers participate in relationships: they see relationships not as equal partnerships but as resource factories. Because of their tendency to selfishly prioritize meeting their own needs, they often exploit relationships to extract what they want from the people around them.

This sense of entitlement leads to the sharp undercutting and fits of rage that many abusers are given to. If they can't get their own way they'll often retaliate, whether openly or secretly. Jesus said, "The mouth speaks what the heart is full of. A good man brings good things out of the good stored up in him, and an evil man brings evil things out of the evil stored up in him" (Matthew 12:34–35). How a person chooses to speak and behave is a representation of what their heart is full of, whether good or evil. No one causes or forces them to behave as they do.

Like a boa constrictor squeezes its prey, an abuser uses words and tactics to pressure a victim into fulfilling their personal desires.

Their aggressive (or passive-aggressive) behaviors are all evidence of a heart lusting to acquire what it wants at any cost.

Each of us is accountable to God for our priorities in life and the choices we make from them, whether we feel someone "made us do it" or not. Second Corinthians 5:10 says, "We must all appear before the judgment seat of Christ, so that each of us may receive what is due us for the things done while in the body, whether good or bad." Back in the garden, Adam tried to blame Eve for his choice to eat the fruit of the tree. Though Adam attempted to use Eve as a cover for his shame, God wasn't having it—Adam still received the consequences of his actions.

Speaking of shame, it's at the heart of this entire discussion about priorities. Shame causes all of us to hide, to use all kinds of distractions and vices to cover our inadequacies. Shame is that feeling that says, *I am a mistake.* Whether abusers are aware or not, they are often consumed with deep shame. But rather than reveal their weaknesses and receive the freedom that comes through repentance, they choose to use relationships as a means to manufacture adoration and significance. The word *shame* would be a good substitute for the phrase "worldly sorrow" in 2 Corinthians 7:10 above, since shame also "brings death" and causes utter destruction in our souls and in our relationships.

On the flip side, the word *guilt* would be a good substitute for the phrase "godly sorrow" in the same passage—it "leads to salvation and leaves no regret." Guilt says, *I made a mistake.* So if, for example, you've reacted to abuse by yelling back and name-calling, it's healthy and right to feel disappointed and reflect on better ways to respond to the aggression coming your way. Hear me say this: it is okay to be angry when someone hurts you. This kind of anger is not a sin. But what we do in anger can be a sin, and we can see anger as a warning to take shelter instead of engaging in the fight. But godly sorrow, or guilt, causes us to choose another path, and in changing the way we do things we experience life and closeness with God.

Abuse thrives on the humiliation of shame, where the victim comes to believe they are at least partially responsible for the abuse and therefore remains under the abuser's power. What's more, abusers are often able to convert your healthy guilt over mistakes into toxic shame as they degrade your character for having been so foolish or selfish in the first place. As you heal from the emotional torment you've endured, it's essential that you begin to pick out the lies of shame as they creep into your mind. They are the ultimate stronghold and a major barrier to emotional freedom for many victims.

Be wary: when you look to separate yourself from the situation, abusers will often become even bolder in their shaming of you. Abusers may try to implicate you, detailing every fault and failure (whether real or imagined). They will do this either to draw you back into the fight or to gain the advantage in getting others to believe their story. This is known as a "smear campaign."[4] Don't be fooled and don't waste your energy crafting a counterresponse; it only gives weight to a false argument and plays into their bid for power.

God promises justice. First Peter 4:3–5 says, "You have spent enough time in the past doing what pagans choose to do . . . They are surprised that you do not join them in their reckless, wild living, and they heap abuse on you. But they will have to give account to him who is ready to judge the living and the dead."

The past is gone. There may be some things you've done or words you've said in response to the mistreatment you've received that you wish you could take back. But it doesn't mean that the abuse you've suffered is at all your fault or that you should be shamed into giving someone another chance.

Reflection and Prayer

Do you have the tendency to take the blame? What lies have caused you to feel responsible for the mistreatment you've endured? How have your responses kept the cycle spinning? How would you like to change that?

In your time with God, consider asking Him to stir your heart for the life He has for you. Ask Him to help you resist attacks you may face in distancing yourself from hurtful relationships and to guide you in responding well.

IT'S NOT PERSONAL

> Our struggle is not against flesh and blood, but against the rulers, against the authorities, against the powers of this dark world and against the spiritual forces of evil in the heavenly realms. Therefore put on the full armor of God, so that when the day of evil comes, you may be able to stand your ground, and after you have done everything, to stand.
> **EPHESIANS 6:12–13**

It's hard to imagine that someone who was supposed to love and protect you (and maybe even said they would) could do such atrocious things. It might even make you wonder, *Was I not good enough?*

You may be experiencing a broad range of emotions as you try to make sense of all this: anger, rejection, shame, sadness, disappointment, and even longing—longing to be seen and heard.

In this longing, you may feel a deep need for closure, to have your experience validated by the one who hurt you. Sometimes we sense that if they could just hear us out, it would prove that we had some value in their eyes, that our time with them was not wasted. But this places your healing and your ability to move on in the hands of your abuser, and it hands your power right back to the one who has tried to strip it from you all along.

But you can still make peace with what has happened to you by recognizing that your abuse did not have anything to do with you specifically as a person. Not one thing. A person who chooses abusive means to engage in relationships simply seeks an unsuspecting target whom they feel they can break down, guilt-trip, and coerce to get what they want. They use the good times to rack up points for themselves that they can cash in when the bad times hit, to "remind" you of their good deeds and keep you from leaving. While you may have felt that you had some good times and some bad times, the reality is that with an abuser, all of it is meant to work together to form one giant, elaborate manipulation.

Whether or not you felt chosen, admired, or special at one time (not everyone does, but many who have been targets of abuse do), abusers are selective about whom they seek to control. And while they may choose a target because that person is special (think *trophy*), they mostly choose them because they are *available*. Vulnerable. And if the target hadn't been you, it would have been (and perhaps already has been or will be) someone else.

That doesn't mean you aren't special; you absolutely are. You are exceptionally made, and purely by virtue of your standing as a child of God, your personhood is imbued with worth and dignity that is to be celebrated (Psalm 139:14–16). Honored. Cherished. But all that means nothing to an abuser, because it has nothing to do with them. Beyond what they can get from you, they can't perceive of your inherent and intrinsic value, which is why they can't properly appreciate or respect it.

There's nothing you can do, say, or be to be "enough" for someone who is set on using and objectifying other people to satisfy their needs and desires. The appetite of an abusive person is insatiable as they go about life seeking what's new and novel to fill the gaping hole within their hearts. The truth is, each of us has a God-shaped hole at the core of our essence meant only to be filled by God Himself. Nothing—not another person, not possessions, not addictions—can fill it the way only He can. Everything else will leave us wanting.

Abusers choose illegitimate means to fill legitimate needs. They opt for greed over grace. They crave power instead of peace. They are trapped in a perpetual state of want as they look to the things of the world that gratify rather than to the things of God that edify. They settle for what is easy over what is good, what is instant over what endures. While in this state, they are unable to participate in a healthy relationship that requires an others-serving kind of love because they are so consumed with a self-serving kind of lust.

James 1:14–15 says, "Each person is tempted when they are dragged away by their own evil desire and enticed. Then, after desire has conceived, it gives birth to sin; and sin, when it is full-grown, gives birth to death." God designed our hearts to be truly filled only by His love. His love is life itself. But a heart that settles for the cheap and temporary substitute of lust becomes infected with sin, which eventually brings forth death. A person who is not actively working against lust is inviting the devil to work inside them. When that happens, you're not merely dealing with a flesh-and-blood human being; you are engaging in a spiritual battle with the powers of darkness.

When it comes to the spiritual war, Satan uses all kinds of tricks and traps to distract you with a toxic relationship so you never see the bigger game he's playing. While your thoughts are spinning over what is going on with this other person, the enemy is making sure your wonderfully creative heart and mind don't get anywhere near the life God originally created you for. The possibilities for your life are endless, and the enemy knows it. What better way for him to defeat you than simply to keep you walking around in circles, questioning yourself, and trying to make sense of nonsense?

Jesus told us that the battle would come and that it would be played out in our relationships—even with the people we're closest to. He said in Matthew 10:34–36:

> "Do not suppose that I have come to bring peace to the earth. I did not come to bring peace, but a sword. For I have come to turn 'a man against his father, a daughter against her mother, a daughter-in-law against her mother-in-law—a man's enemies will be the members of his own household.'"

What do you do when the war that rages is within yourself? On one hand, you may have enough resolve to begin confronting an unhealthy situation. Yet it seems the moment you do, doubt creeps in, causing you to wonder if you're really doing the right thing. This push and pull is a normal part of the liberation process; Satan does not let go without a fight. Think of how in the book of Exodus, Pharaoh let God's people go only to chase them down as soon as they'd left. Moses' words to the Israelites in that moment ring true in this moment of your life as well; in Exodus 14:14 he says, "The LORD will fight for you; you need only to be still." The word "still" in this context means "quiet" or "silent," but in such a courageous way that instead of turning back, you can stand steadfast as God confirms the truth of the situation and reveals the way out.

You may not feel very courageous on many parts of this journey. But courage doesn't mean the absence of fear; rather, it's the ability to stand in the face of it. If God has granted you enough clarity to know even a glimmer of the truth, He will deliver you the rest of the way. He's doing the heavy work. When you don't know what to do, that's a good time to be still and wait on Him.

Reflection and Prayer

How have you gotten distracted fighting the wrong enemy? Has doubt caused you to second-guess what has already been revealed to you? How can you embrace what it means to be still and allow God to fight for you?

In your time with God, consider asking Him to show you the truth about the spiritual battle you are engaged in. Seek His relief for what you have suffered, and ask for His guidance in learning to be still as He fights for you.

SECTION 2

The Hiding Place

You hide them in the shelter of your presence, safe from those who conspire against them. You shelter them in your presence, far from accusing tongues.

PSALM 31:20 (NLT)

I grew up near San Francisco, California. One of my all-time favorite school field trips was to Alcatraz Island, home of the infamous maximum security penitentiary. I vividly remember walking down the ominous cell block corridors, clutching a black-and-yellow Walkman as I listened to the guided tour on cassette tape. The guide (who sounded like he could have been narrating a horror film) detailed the stories of desperate prisoners who sought to escape their abysmal fate stuck out on "the Rock." And while several men succeeded in slipping past the guards, their hopes of escape were inevitably dashed when they hit the craggy shores of the island, which plummeted into the unforgiving waters of frigid San Francisco Bay. Despite having escaped, with nowhere to go these men were never truly free.

Escape without a place of refuge leaves the escapee vulnerable and exposed. When God frees us from abuse, it's not like an ill-conceived Alcatraz prison break. God's desire is not to remove the abused from their oppression only to leave them stranded on the shores. He intends for our souls to experience true freedom under the complete covering of His protection.

Psalm 91:1 says, "Whoever dwells in the shelter of the Most High will rest in the shadow of the Almighty." That word "shelter" in the original Hebrew literally means something more like "hiding place." We can find rest for our souls in God's protection because God's shadow falls over us and hides us completely.

Psalm 91:4 likens it to huddling under the wing of a bird. It says, "He will cover you with his feathers, and under his wings you will find refuge; his faithfulness will be your shield and rampart."

Let me stop here for a second. When I considered this verse in the past, I'd get the mental picture of a plump mother hen nurturing a flock of peeping hatchlings beneath her wings. But as I dug deeper, I discovered that's not the imagery Psalm 91 is drawing upon. The greater context of this passage is nudging us to experience God as a mighty eagle, a regal bird of prey.

Eagles are dominant, aggressive, and more strategic than other winged creatures. Eagles are known to build impressive nests, called aeries, high upon treacherous cliff faces. The diameter of the average aerie is six to ten feet across, with walls six to ten feet high.[5] Seems like overkill for a creature with razor-sharp talons and a death grip nearly ten times stronger than that of a human. But eagles take defense just as seriously as offense. And that's the image God wants us to have of His protection of us.

We can see this same language elsewhere in the Bible. Job 5:11 says, "The lowly he sets on high, and those who mourn are lifted to safety." The word for "safety" here describes being lifted so inaccessibly high as to ensure complete victory and prosperity. Imagine God as a powerful eagle, lifting you up into His fortified aerie, out of view from your enemies as He covers you and fights for you.

So much more than a plump mother hen can do.

If abuse you've suffered has caused you to doubt God, distrust Him, or shy away from Him, you're not alone. If your experiences have made you feel as though He's disappointed, or demanding, or that you need to work hard to make Him approve of you, know that that's also common. But, dear one, God isn't threatened by any of that. Even in your uncertainty, He is perfectly patient and steady. He awaits you still. He invites you to unearth all that has kept you from knowing Him as He truly is and to place it all in His capable hands.

Throughout your recovery experience, you may find yourself asking God, "Can You—will You—love the real me?" In my doubting and questioning, I feared I would anger God or that He would become frustrated with me. On the contrary, God revealed more of His kindness and goodness to me in my doubts, not less. He held me close, not at arm's length. He showed me that in doubt, we may start asking Him the kinds of questions that lead us to knowing and trusting Him more. I pray that as you bring yourself to Him completely, as you are without pretense, you will sense Him enveloping you in safety and acceptance. I pray you'll begin to experience God as your hiding place and uncommon respite for your weary soul, body, and spirit.

Within this invitation lies a choice: turning toward safety means turning away from everything you've known, and that can be frightening. Proverbs 27:12 puts the choice this way: "The prudent see danger and take refuge, but the simple keep going and pay the penalty." Trusting God's leading isn't always easy, but the alternatives and shortcuts won't take you where you really want to go.

In the hiding place, we wrestle with the hard questions in safety, and we learn to shift our dependency onto a tender and patient God so we can find rest and refuge for our souls. The focus on this part of your healing path is twofold: learning to turn away from what has hurt you while simultaneously learning to turn toward God. At times this will feel like a welcomed relief, while other times you may find yourself challenged and frustrated by the process and complex emotions. But God has time and compassion for you in your healing. He is not in a rush. And against the backdrop of this ever-changing life, God offers you a lasting sense of stability and security that only He, in His unchanging nature, can provide.

> You are my hiding place;
> you will protect me from trouble
> and surround me with
> songs of deliverance.
>
> PSALM 32:7

8

WHY DID THIS HAPPEN?

> We do not lose heart. Though outwardly we are wasting away, yet inwardly we are being renewed day by day.
> **2 CORINTHIANS 4:16**

Wasting away. Dealing with the suffering caused by abuse can feel just like that. Energy wasted. Time wasted. Tears wasted. You may even feel that you've become a version of yourself that you don't even recognize anymore. Trauma does that to a person—it can cause you to shrink down and hold back, never truly exploring or celebrating who you really are.

This is a kind of suffering that degrades us. It seeks to destroy our understanding of what it is to be made in the image of God, in the *imago Dei*. It's a low blow from the enemy who knows just what wonderful creatures we'll become if given the opportunity to flourish in our God-given uniqueness and power.

We often feel a sense that things aren't supposed to be this way. God didn't design the world or our relationships this way. But in knowing this, many victims ask, "Why, then, did God allow this to happen to me?"

Many theologians (and other people a whole lot smarter than me) have wrestled with the mysteries of suffering for centuries. And to be honest, when it comes to my human experience, I've not heard an explanation so far that has made any measurable difference in lessening the weight of my sorrow.

I don't get hung up on looking for the answers because they just aren't enough in times like this. The hurt just hurts, and there's no way around that. But even without answers, we can still find some solace to carry us—not around, but through.

Here's what we do know: our world is fallen, it's the devil who caused it, and he's been trying to blame God ever since. Just as with Eve, the devil uses the things we don't understand about life to cause us to doubt God's motives. He does this so we distrust and dodge the only hope we ever have of experiencing healing and restoration.

Think of it this way: he knows you'll never seek help from the Physician if you doubt He even wants you to get well. When bad things happen, the enemy deftly shifts the focus off himself and tries to deceive you into believing

1) God does not give good things; or
2) God may give good things, but they're not for you.

Jesus let us in on Satan's motives in John 10:10 when He said, "The thief comes only to steal and kill and destroy." Satan is out to steal what doesn't belong to him and obliterate whatever's left that he can't have. One of the ways he does this is by taking our very natural questions and filling in the gaps with lies. But to counter these lies, Jesus continues in John 10:10, "I have come that they may have life, and have it to the full."

You are not defective if you have doubt; doubt is a natural part of growing faith. When there are no easy answers, doubt is an opportunity for choice: we can spend our energy seeking certainty, or we can move forward in the face of the unknown.

The enemy wants you to experience doubt in a way that extends your suffering. He knows if the lies speak loudly enough, you'll shy away from God. If he can convince you to shrink away, he knows he can keep you from the part of your story where the renewing takes place, where you begin to experience life to the full. If he can cause you to lose heart halfway through, he knows you will never see the glory of the comeback that awaits you in the second act.

But really, doubt can be an open door to seeing God for *who* He is, as He does what He says He can do. When we struggle to take Him at His word, God does not shame us but rather invites us to know Him in real life through what we can watch Him do with our suffering.

The power in moving beyond pain is in realizing you still have a choice: Will you allow it to break you or remake you? If you want to move forward, you have a critical decision to make. Can you shift the focus away from *why* this happened to *what* God will do with it?

John 9 offers an indelible example of understanding the difference between the *why* and the *what*. In this passage, Jesus and His disciples encountered a man, blind from birth, on the side of the road. At the outset, the disciples quickly became preoccupied with the *why* behind this man's suffering. They asked Jesus in verse 2, "Rabbi, who sinned, this man or his parents, that he was born blind?"

Jesus answered the disciples' question, but not in the way they expected. Jesus gently explained in verse 3, "Neither this man nor his parents sinned . . . but this happened so that the works of God might be displayed in him." What Jesus alludes to here is not so much the *why* behind this man's suffering as the *what*—what God would reveal about Himself and His goodness in the situation. Jesus pointed the disciples away from the past and toward the potential of the present.

Jesus healed the man, and while his physical blindness was cured, what God granted him was so much greater than that. This man, once an outcast beggar deemed worthless by mainstream society, was restored to a completely new level of physical, spiritual, *and* emotional wholeness. In making him the living, breathing evidence of a miracle, Jesus effectively delivered him out of social obscurity and into the pages of redemption history.

And the man's suffering was the catalyst for it all.

I love the fact that the blind man's transformation makes him nearly unrecognizable to those who knew him before. In verses 8–9, his neighbors began asking, "'Isn't this the same man who used to sit and beg?' Some claimed that he was. Others said, 'No, he only looks like him.' But he himself insisted, 'I am the man.'" The blind man had been so radically changed, people literally could not believe it. I can attest to that in my own life; my own transformation has made me unrecognizable in the best ways.

Asking "why?" is a fair question, but it's not where the power of healing and transformation is found. "Why" keeps you looking backward, staring at your circumstances and stuck in the suffering. This is precisely where the enemy wants you, so you will avoid stepping into your God-given destiny. In the devil's hands, suffering *deforms* you, pulling you apart and making you less than what God intends.

But asking "what" keeps you curious about what God is still doing, and dares you to take even one step forward and into the future to see what could happen. Suffering placed in God's hands *transforms* you and makes you into something new. Believing God has something for you beyond brokenness opens your heart and mind to receive and experience His healing power in your life. And in the process, you become so much more—more confident, more empowered, more free.

God's presence in our pain ultimately gives our suffering meaning and purpose, not the answers to a thousand "whys." And as we later bask in the total miracle of transformation, the reasons why things happened become so much less interesting than what God has done through it all.

I know, easy for me to say. But God is doing the same thing right now in the middle of your own story, even if you don't quite see it yet. So while you walk and while you wait, you can know this: the healing is coming. "For our light and momentary troubles are achieving for us an eternal glory that far outweighs them all. So we fix our eyes not on what is seen, but on what is unseen, since what is seen is temporary, but what is unseen is eternal" (2 Corinthians 4:17–18).

Reflection and Prayer

What has the enemy tried to steal, kill, or destroy in you? How has what you've suffered caused you to become less than what God made you to be?

In your prayer time, consider asking God to show you what He will do with all you have suffered. Share your frustration, sorrow, and grief with Him. Ask Him to help you learn to rest in the comfort of His coming glory.

9

NO ESCAPE

> Look at the birds of the air; they do not sow or reap or store away in barns, and yet your heavenly Father feeds them. Are you not much more valuable than they? Can any one of you by worrying add a single hour to your life?
> **MATTHEW 6:26–27**

When you remove an unhealthy relationship from your life, it leaves a gaping hole. It's often not until the abusive person is gone that we realize how much time, energy, and effort we've spent trying to make a bad thing good. After an experience like that, it's normal to feel disappointed, disenchanted, and dejected.

All kinds of things seem to offer us an out to fill in that hole and escape the pain, though not all of them are good. I've found that the ones that come to us most easily are often the worst—though it may not appear that way on the surface. Maybe it's endless hours spent reading and researching, looking for one more thing that could fix all this. Perhaps it's emotionally venting without ever really getting anywhere (which feels gratifying in the way poking a bruise does). Or it could be one more bottle, one more puff, one more relationship, one more work commitment, one more snacking binge, or one more shopping spree—

anything to feel something other than the pain (or to feel nothing at all).

You'll get no judgment from me on this. I've been there too.

These obsessions and addictions seem to offer us some solace because they give us the illusion of choice. They offer us a false sense of control over our lives, when in reality they are just another thing to become enslaved by.

I know these things can be well-intended. When you've focused so much attention on someone who took advantage of you, it can feel empowering to give something to yourself. And hear me say this—that's definitely a good thing and essential to the healing process (more on that in a bit). But when a habit is used to escape from the deep work of acknowledging your feelings and healing, you'll find the problems compounded in the long run.

If you look back on those who have hurt you, you may see a common thread. Kind words were always laced with criticism, affection was forced or withheld, or gifts were given with strings attached (if they were given at all). As a result, you may have learned to cope with life with some combination of overgiving and disconnection from your own needs. Relationships seem so much safer if you're the one doing all the giving, and you can minimize potential disappointment if you don't need anything in the first place.

These survival skills protect us from relationships that are unsafe; if we shut our hearts down and emphasize giving, it might prevent us from receiving anything harmful. But these protective strategies also keep us from receiving anything good.

While Jesus did say it is "more blessed to give than to receive," in that simple expression He implies that receiving is still blessed too (Acts 20:35). But the practice of receiving can be unenjoyable and perhaps even threatening when we are recovering from abuse because to completely receive you must allow your heart to be open.

Opening your heart requires vulnerability. It means sharing your hopes, failures, dreams, and sorrows, which are all inextricably tied. And while God designed healthy relationships to be places where we could safely express our vulnerabilities and experience the healing found in mutual giving and receiving, engaging with other people in that way can be too difficult at first. I certainly had my share of misses, trusting my heart with people I should not have. It was enough to make me want to remain "safe" and shut down. But in every failure, God gently turned my eyes toward Himself. And in all my crying, complaining, praising, and petitioning, God gave me a very real awareness of His compassion for me. I felt *seen, heard*.

Eventually I craved spending time with Him. I found myself enjoying Him. And instead of feeling depleted, I started feeling like I really had something to offer, something to give. But it wasn't coupled with the rejection of my needs anymore; it was out of the overflow of having my need for acceptance and belonging perfectly met.

There's something frightening about receiving from God when receiving from people has been painful. Sometimes we turn first to what's comfortable, even if it's bad for us, because it's *familiar*. But God does not give in the way that humans give. In John 14:27 Jesus says, "Peace I leave with you; my peace I give you. I do not give to you as the world gives. Do not let your hearts be troubled and do not be afraid."

The world gives in a way that causes anxiety, while God gives in a way that cures it. Receiving may feel somewhat strange at first—perhaps even selfish or uncomfortable. But in a healing season it's essential to receive and experience the delight God has in you, the joy He has at the very thought of you. When you sense that, you'll find it easier to treat yourself in the same way, to delight in the creation that you are and return the attention you've been spending on the people who have wounded you back to yourself instead.

Receiving love from God and offering it to yourself is not selfish, nor does it mean you are neglecting anyone else. First John 4:19 says, "We love because he first loved us." The fact is we can't give the love that we haven't first received and enjoyed. As you journey through the months ahead, be sure to take time each day to practice soaking up the love God has for you in even the smallest things you observe and experience in your daily life.

Understandably, the fear of disappointment is a real threat to this process, especially when you've been hurt before. The enemy uses people to hurt us and then manipulates those experiences to keep us from exposing our pain and receiving healing from a generous and gentle Father. The enemy knows what you'll become if you open your heart to receive God's restorative blessings, and he'll do anything to stop you.

God desires life for *you*—one that is overflowing with perfect peace—and He is working through your circumstances to see that you get it. If God is not giving you what you're desperate for in this season, don't despair—He's not holding out on you. God doesn't give like people do, and He doesn't play games to see if you have enough faith. Through the gifts He gives, He teaches us how to receive from Him in ways that strengthen our dependence on Him and elevate our faith. Rest assured He has something good for you and a better, more complete way of healing and restoring you.

As Jesus said in Matthew 7:11, "If you sinful people know how to give good gifts to your children, how much more will your heavenly Father give good gifts to those who ask him" (NLT). Perhaps what you've been asking for or chasing after will keep you stuck in a cycle of bondage when God really wants to see you set free in every way possible. When you open your heart and mind to the possibilities, you'll see His love move in your life in ways you never imagined.

Reflection and Prayer

What coping strategies have given you a sense of escape? In what ways are you afraid to open your heart to God?

In your prayer time, consider asking God to help you with opening up your heart. Tell Him about any fears you have about being vulnerable. Cry out to Him about the mistreatment you've received and how difficult it has made it to open your heart. Ask Him to give you strength to keep going in the uncertain rather than settling for what you can see and understand.

10

FACING FORWARD

> Not that I have already obtained all this, or have already arrived at my goal, but I press on to take hold of that for which Christ Jesus took hold of me. Brothers and sisters, I do not consider myself yet to have taken hold of it. But one thing I do: Forgetting what is behind and straining toward what is ahead, I press on toward the goal to win the prize for which God has called me heavenward in Christ Jesus.
> **PHILIPPIANS 3:12–14**

The point of rescue is also a point of no return—a point when you look at where you've come from and realize you can't ever go back. In one sense, it feels altogether liberating; the relief that comes from long-awaited deliverance is like one great, big, deep exhale. Yet in another sense, it's unnerving; freedom is unfamiliar, and it often carries with it waves of guilt, exhaustion, anger, anxiety, and sadness, among many other emotions. Though these feelings often change quickly and collide in conflict, they are all valuable and valid in their own ways.

At times, the unfamiliarity of freedom may tempt you to renegotiate the terms of separation in an effort to cope with the pain of losing a significant relationship and the life that accompanied it. Often this can look like questioning the choice to separate from someone who has been hurting you. You might be dreaming of all the good times you had with this person and wondering if maybe you are "the crazy one" or if it wasn't as bad as you thought. You might be tempted to relax your boundaries and allow the person to come close to you again without them having done the necessary work. It can also look like taking too much responsibility for what's happened and proactively reconciling the relationship without the necessary proof of repentance on their part.

I say this with absolute compassion for you as you wrestle with this tension: anything you do to reengage with someone you've had to distance yourself from is a step straight back toward what God is rescuing you from. The Israelites did this very thing just before crossing the Red Sea in Exodus 14. In verse 12, they complained to Moses, "Didn't we say to you in Egypt, 'Leave us alone; let us serve the Egyptians'? It would have been better for us to serve the Egyptians than to die in the desert!"

Serve the Egyptians? Generations of Israelites were brutally exploited by their Egyptian enslavers—there was no serving going on here. Yet out of the Israelites' fear of the unknown, they ended up minimizing and recategorizing the treatment they'd received to justify going back.

One reason the Israelites were so willing to distort their view of what they were being saved from was they didn't have a grasp of what they were being saved *for*. Despite God's promise to lead them to a land of plenty, they didn't yet have a vision so compelling that they'd be willing to endure whatever it took to get to the other side. One short stint in the desert and they'd already decided there was no way they could be heading into anything better than what they'd left behind.

It's not so different with us. It's easier to focus on the known (even if it's not so good) and try to make that work than to have hope in the face of the unknown. Rescue requires learning to live in a new way, which can feel like wandering through the desert. It is lonely, frustrating, and disorienting.

Letting go of the past does not mean it never mattered. Your past matters to God; nothing you've gone through will be wasted, and He is working through it to bring forth good (Romans 8:28). But transformation requires releasing an old thing to make room for a new one. When you loosen your grip on the outcome of a situation, you're freed up to experience what God would do through it. You start to see things more like He sees them.

God says through the prophet Isaiah: "My thoughts are not your thoughts, neither are your ways my ways . . . As the heavens are higher than the earth, so are my ways higher than your ways and my thoughts than your thoughts" (Isaiah 55:8–9).

Whatever God desires for you, He will make known to you in due season. In the meantime, don't limit yourself to what you see and understand, and don't make the whole process harder on yourself by running back toward the past. God's not taking you that way. Instead, look toward the future, expecting that the goodness that carried you out of oppression is the same goodness that's carrying you into a new life of liberty.

Reflection and Prayer

In what ways might you be holding on to the past in your life? What do you need to release to receive what God wants to do in the future?

In your time with God, consider asking Him to bring you comfort and clarity in the midst of an unfamiliar season. Ask Him to give you wisdom to see things as He does and the strength of heart to move in that direction.

11

BOUNDARIES

> He has saved us and called us to a holy life—not because of anything we have done but because of his own purpose and grace. This grace was given us in Christ Jesus before the beginning of time.
> **2 TIMOTHY 1:9**

What comes to mind when you think of the word *holy*? We know God is holy and He calls us to be holy, but what does that even mean?

The word *holy* means "set apart." When I think of "set apart," I think of that favored slice of birthday cake you set aside for the birthday boy or girl (which in my case was usually the corner piece with the extra frosting). It's hand selected and specifically reserved for the enjoyment of the one it was made for. It's not unlike our relationship with God. When He saved you through Jesus' death and resurrection, He set you apart—simply because it delighted Him to do so.

As we've discussed before, we are likely to become like the people we associate with, and toxic people have a tendency to distract us from our purpose and stunt our personal growth. But to mature into the people God has called us to become, we all need to be around other people who are seeking the very same thing. That's why 2 Corinthians 6:14 instructs, "Do not be yoked together with unbelievers. For what do righteousness and wickedness have in common? Or what fellowship can light have with darkness?"

Being "yoked together" means "joined up with." In this verse, Paul was referring to anyone who has significant influence in your life or vice versa, whether that's a spouse, close friend or family member, or even a business partner. Paul stressed the importance of being linked up with people who are both committed to the Lord and growing in that commitment, for purposes of your sanctity—*and* your sanity.

To Paul, being attached to a spiritually immature person made as much sense as fresh eggs being in the same carton as rotten ones.

Think of it this way: In the three-legged race of life, where we are all joined together and running toward Jesus at the finish line, are the people you are running with putting in an effort equal to yours? Or have you been dragging some individuals along, hoping they'll eventually get with it?

Just as you must assess yourself to know where you are in your own spiritual growth, you must carefully conduct the same assessment of the people around you. That's what it means to ensure you are not unequally yoked. So often when we are in relationships with people who are hurting us, we find that we have

1) not done this assessment;
2) assessed others according to what we want to see rather than what's really there; or
3) given people too much access and influence in our lives for their level of spiritual commitment and maturity.

Ephesians 2:10 says you are "God's masterpiece" and that "He has created [you] anew in Christ Jesus, so [you] can do the good things he planned for [you] long ago" (NLT). Imagine God as an artisan, skillfully crafting your unique personhood long before you were born. He delighted in creating you and then selected good things for you to do with your precious life while on this earth. The last thing He wants is to see His fantastic creation damaged by a careless individual who cares nothing about your original design or purpose.

You are set apart.

It may seem wrong to judge and distance yourself from another person, but Paul describes the process plainly in 1 Corinthians 5:12–13. He says, "It isn't my responsibility to judge outsiders, but it certainly is your responsibility to judge those inside the church who are sinning. God will judge those on the outside; but as the Scriptures say, 'You must remove the evil person from among you'" (NLT).

I know you might be thinking, *But aren't we all sinning?* Yes. But the point Paul is trying to make is that some among us are sinning unabashedly against the brethren, intentionally creating divisiveness within the body of Christ and distorting God's harmonious design for His people. The church and our relationships are meant to be places where we can be honest and vulnerable, and it's unsafe for us to open our lives to anyone who would exploit that as an avenue to satiate themselves.

Healthy boundaries are less about building a wall to keep people out and more about honoring and cultivating what is special and sacred within you. Just as we have doors and windows on our houses to keep damaging weather out, they can be opened to bring refreshing breezes in for the enjoyment of the people inside. As we've covered before, creating distance with an unsafe person is not meant to condemn them. But boundaries do honor God's intention from the beginning of time to set you apart by His delight while preventing you from being corrupted by harmful influences.

We can uphold healthy boundaries with kindness, firmness, and humility, without a drawn-out explanation. When you do have to set them, typically the shorter and more direct you are in your communication, the better. This definitely takes practice, but it gets easier every time you do it. When you express your boundaries, it is not an opportunity for negotiation and it's not an open door to conversation about the situation. Communicating boundaries is about delineating what you have predetermined you will or won't do in the future. The process is more about your future action than their past behavior. Most simply put, you are just not headed in the same direction at the same speed, and you are gently releasing them to God's care while you pursue a life of peace.

Your distinct personhood matters to God, and He desires to see you thrive in it. First and foremost, He created you to delight in Him so He could delight in you. Your human relationships are meant to aid you in experiencing that to the greatest degree possible because "you are a chosen people, a royal priesthood, a holy nation, God's special possession, that you may declare the praises of him who called you out of darkness into his wonderful light" (1 Peter 2:9).

Reflection and Prayer

How have unhealthy relationships kept you from growing into the person God made you to be? How can you change this to put more emphasis on discovering your unique identity and enjoying God?

In your time with God, consider asking Him for new insight and fresh inspiration as it relates to His unique design of you. Ask Him to fill you with a sense of His delight in you and to guide you in growing closer to people who will help model and uphold good boundaries.

12

THE FREEDOM OF FORGIVENESS

> If it is possible, as far as it depends on you, live at peace with everyone. Do not take revenge, my dear friends, but leave room for God's wrath, for it is written: "It is mine to avenge; I will repay," says the Lord.
> **ROMANS 12:18–19**

So often what connects a victim to an abuser is compassion. You may have a keen awareness of your abuser's early wounds and traumas, and you may have felt stirred with compassion for what they've suffered. So many survivors, myself included, say they felt a sense of responsibility toward their abuser—to be a source of kindness in an unkind world.

That word *compassion* is interesting because it literally means "to suffer with."[6] The *com* part means "with." It's where we get words like *community* and *combine*. Strikingly, that means then that the word *passion* carries with it, when on its own, the meaning of "suffer."

And that's what the emotional experience of separating from an abuser often feels like—compassion turned to isolated suffering. As the truth is unmasked and you're left on your own, you may find the compassion you felt for that person is replaced by an equally powerful passion against them. And as you begin to recount all the times your love and compassion were taken for granted and used against you, you may find yourself extremely angry.

You must know that your anger is a good thing. Anger can be a righteous and right reaction to injustice; God Himself is angered by injustice. As we've said before, anger itself is not a sin but rather an emotion God has given you to alert you to something that needs your attention. Anger is not always immediate, and it can come when you least expect it. You may find memories resurfacing at the strangest times, accompanied by feelings of fierce rage. God designed our brains to suppress negative experiences to help us cope with overwhelming stress. But when the threat is minimized and the stress reduces, it's not uncommon to find yourself flooded with thoughts and feelings (even in your sleep). And while the experience is unpleasant, it's your brain's way of letting you know that you are ready for the next step in your healing journey.

Anger can be righteous, but as imperfect humans our reactions to anger can be anything but. You may be prone to holding grudges, gossiping, retaliating, or deflecting to avoid your emotions altogether. In any case, if you're not intentional about digging out the real root causes, sooner or later what started as a manageable flame can turn into a destructive inferno.

Anger is a normal reaction to sin, but it can also cause it. Ephesians 4:26–27 says, "'In your anger do not sin': Do not let the sun go down while you are still angry, and do not give the devil a foothold." Anger has a shelf life, and it has to be dealt with; otherwise anger gives Satan a foothold in your heart, and he uses that anger to stir up sin. Anger might feel justified for a time, but if it turns to sin, it will ultimately rob you of your freedom. And the only way to experience true freedom from all this pain and anger is forgiveness.

God's forgiveness of your sins sets you free from the bondage of your own sin; your forgiveness of another person sets you free from the bondage of theirs. Think about it this way: sin is infectious. Someone in your abuser's past no doubt inflicted hurt upon them. That sin has infected your abuser's heart, and as it has incubated, they have chosen to react in ways that pass that sickness on to you. Should you choose to let their sin birth sin within you, you will not only find yourself tethered to their sin but will risk spreading it to the people you love. You owe it to yourself to stop the madness and cut yourself off from that—to give yourself and your loved ones a new legacy.

Like it or not (and probably not), you are connected to your abuser through the injury you've sustained at their hands. Forgiving your abuser cuts that tie and releases you to pursue life unbound. Forgiveness doesn't mean that what they did didn't happen; forgiveness says you are done carrying it around and that you're leaving the consequences of that person's sin in God's hands to avenge. It means you are opening your hands to let go of pain and in its place receive peace.

Colossians 1:20 says God "[reconciled] to himself all things, whether things on earth or things in heaven, by making peace through [Jesus'] blood, shed on the cross." The death and resurrection of Jesus secured our forgiveness, and as a result, God has made peace with us. The Old Testament word we often translate as "peace" is *shalom*. But *shalom* means so much more than peace—it's well-being and harmony, wholeness and oneness with God. God's forgiveness of our sins through Jesus was His means of restoring shalom to us, and you experience shalom more deeply in the process of forgiving others. It may not seem like it in the moment, but that's only because forgiveness happens before healing begins.

Forgiveness isn't a feeling; it's a choice. It's not a betrayal of yourself or a denial of what you've suffered. In fact, forgiveness requires you to first acknowledge what was done to you and how it has affected you, so you have a full understanding of what you are asking God to repair and make right. Then, in forgiving the person who has harmed you, you in effect separate yourself from them and invite God to deal with the situation on your behalf as you exit the scene.

In forgiveness, we take God at His word and trust Him to repay what has been stolen, as He has promised. When you give up your own way of finding justice, you also get to give up the corrosive anger and searing bitterness that threatens the shalom that Jesus has already secured for you.

Let me be clear: forgiving someone will not always lead to reconciliation, nor should it. Forgiveness unlocks the door to reconciliation, but as we've discussed before, repentance is required to open it. Again, in Matthew 18 Jesus said, "If your brother or sister sins, go and point out their fault, just between the two of you. If they listen to you, you have won them over" (v. 15). Key in on that phrase "if they listen to you." Jesus is clear here that reconciliation requires the offending party to listen and take genuine responsibility for their wrongdoing. But He makes allowance for the fact that in their free will, they may decide not to do so.

If you fear reconciling with an abusive person, there's nothing wrong with you. It doesn't mean anything is wrong with your faith; it means you know this person is not trustworthy. Forgiveness does not repair trust, and mutual trust is required to maintain relationships. Reconciliation and restoration are not possible, nor are they biblically advisable, when dealing with a person who hasn't demonstrated real remorse and trustworthiness. Forgiveness is a free gift you give, but your trust is something to be earned.

Romans 12:18 says, "If it is possible, as far as it depends on you, live at peace with everyone." Living at peace does not mean that you are engaged in relationship again; it means that through forgiveness, you are preventing the disharmony of hatred from threatening the potential for peace. If the person who has hurt you continues to be hurtful or ignore their fault, there's nothing more you can do about that. But as far as it depends on you, you are choosing peace.

Sometimes it's not easy to tell if someone who is abusing you is truly sorry for what they've done. How do you know if you are dealing with true repentance?

Time.

In Matthew 7:20 Jesus says, "Yes, just as you can identify a tree by its fruit, so you can identify people by their actions" (NLT). Trees do not bear fruit overnight and neither does an apologetic abuser. As we've discussed, abuse operates in a cycle, and false apologies are a part of that cycle.

Something to remember: an apology without changed behavior is manipulation.

To determine whether the apology is authentic, you must watch and see if what they say and what they do match over time. In intimate relationships, that means a changed individual will show consistent improvement over months and perhaps years. And that doesn't need to happen in interactions with just you—the fruit of their life will be evident in *all* their dealings. When you are not involved, are they taking it upon themselves to be accountable to God? Or are they replacing their dependence on you with a dependence on other people or things, making it glaringly obvious that you made the right choice? Only consistent, sustained effort over time demonstrates trustworthiness.

Forgiveness can be difficult because it doesn't always feel good. Forgiveness comes before the other person has put in any work and before your emotions have really subsided. But forgiveness allows you to cut yourself off from the source of what's hurt you, and it keeps you from being reinjured by it. The abuser might still do things that are hurtful, and you may still have to forgive them again and again. But don't expect healing to give you the power to forgive; forgiveness gives you the freedom to let go and heal.

Reflection and Prayer

Do you have the tendency to harbor bitterness? Do you move to reconciliation too quickly? How does this discussion of forgiveness make forgiving easier? How does it make it more challenging?

In your time of prayer, consider asking God for the strength to forgive. Ask Him to free you from the chains of sin that you've been bound to and to replace your anger with peace. You can also ask for faith to trust that God will bring about justice and protect you as you wait on Him.

13

DEALING WITH DISCARD

> Above all else, guard your heart, for everything you do flows from it.
> **PROVERBS 4:23**

Separation gives you the necessary time and space to see your situation more clearly, but you may not always like what you observe. Change is difficult, and abusers often avoid it in a variety of ways. It is far easier for an abuser to attempt to convince you that they have changed or persuade you that you're making the wrong move than it is for them to actually do the work. You may even see desperate, grandiose, or tearful attempts to draw you back in (called "hoovering,"[7] like the vacuum). But as you practice holding firm boundaries, the truth always reveals itself. Desperation often turns to vengeance, and you may experience a phenomenon known as "discard."[8]

Discard is when an abuser rejects you and blames you for the breakdown of the relationship. Abusers treat people as objects that provide personal gratification; when you no longer play their manipulative games, they no longer have use for you. To protect their own reputation in the fallout, you may find that they become more aggressive in destroying yours. During the discard phase, they may slander you (something known as a "smear campaign") or they may quickly replace you with another source of admiration. All this is designed to make you angry or jealous; if they can get a reaction out of you, they know they still have some level of control.

Discard is painful. You will wonder how someone who claimed to care for you could just throw you away. Again, none of this is personal. Nothing is wrong with you. This is another level of a twisted game designed to drain you of energy and rob you of your peace.

Guarding your heart is extremely crucial at a time like this. You will begin to experience something like a withdrawal from the relationship as your body begins to detox from the chemical cocktail the brain produces when a person is abused. You may feel like you just can't take it, like you can't live with or without this person in your life. Doubt will become stronger than ever. An unguarded heart is easily deceived, and without boundaries, your anxiety may tempt you to minimize what you've endured and reenter the abusive cycle.

You may be wondering, *How do I guard my heart?* Philippians 4:6–7 says, "Do not be anxious about anything, but in every situation, by prayer and petition, with thanksgiving, present your requests to God. And the peace of God, which transcends all understanding, will guard your hearts and your minds in Christ Jesus." Practically speaking, these verses say that when you feel anxious or confused, you should pray. Pray when your mind is racing. Pray when you are tempted to relax a boundary. Pray when you know you might have to interact with the person who has hurt you. Just tell God you need help and He will give it to you, by way of His peace.

These verses have been so comforting to me in difficult situations. The emotional onslaught of escaping abuse is often incredibly overwhelming, and the thought of having to muster up the strength to guard my own heart sounded exhausting. But these verses remind us that God does the guarding. His peace does the protecting. All I have to do is ask Him for it and remain underneath it. Now, that was something that I could do.

The presence of God's peace eventually grew stronger and stronger, to the point where I no longer feared being deceived. I knew I could see things as they were and that my heart had been stilled to the point that discernment came more naturally. This is critical in the later stages of discard, when you may see bolder attempts on your abuser's part to show off their "new life" without you. It could be a new car, a new house, new friends, a new partner, a big trip—anything that declares, "My life is better now that you're gone."

And why wouldn't they think that life is better without you? There's no one there to hold them accountable anymore!

As you struggle to get by, you may wonder, *Why is this so easy for them? Why does it seem like they are being blessed with everything they want while I suffer?* Psalm 37 addresses this very situation. Verses 7–9 say: Be still before the Lord and wait patiently for him; do not fret when people succeed in their ways, when they carry out their wicked schemes. Refrain from anger and turn from wrath; do not fret—it leads only to evil. For those who are evil will be destroyed, but those who hope in the Lord will inherit the land."

Doing what is right doesn't always feel good. Sometimes it seems totally unfair. But things are never just what they seem. Now that you can identify the discard phase of the abuse cycle, you have the power to see through the ruse and find freedom again in God's protection. God will bring justice at the right time. As Galatians 6:7 says, "Do not be deceived: God cannot be mocked. A man reaps what he sows."

Reflection and Prayer

Have you noticed any signs of being discarded or replaced? How can you understand this as yet another attempt for your abuser to control your emotions?

In your time of prayer, ask God to comfort you through the pain and loss you're experiencing. Seek His peace to cover you as you continue to walk this difficult road, and ask for greater faith to trust that His way is the best way.

14

RESPONDING IN HONOR

"Whoever would love life and see good days must keep their tongue from evil and their lips from deceitful speech. They must turn from evil and do good; they must seek peace and pursue it."
1 PETER 3:10–11

Pursuing peace isn't a passive act. It requires a new kind of commitment and accountability to make changes to the ways you think and act. Even the smallest, seemingly well-intended responses can keep you engaged in an abusive situation without your awareness of it.

Consider this: If your abuser makes a rude remark, how do you typically reply? Do you fire back with an angry counterattack? Do you quietly seethe? Do you try to explain or excuse yourself? Do you try to help them understand? Do you quickly apologize? All these responses are natural responses to trauma, but they are *reactions* that typically keep fear or anger in your driver's seat.

When emotions are running high, it may seem impossible to respond instead of reacting. Second Timothy 1:7 says, "God gave us a spirit not of fear but of power and love and self-control" (ESV). In the original Greek, that word for "fear" has the implication of evil attached to it, meaning that if we operate from fear, we are likely to do or say the wrong thing because of it. That's *reacting*.

But God gives us what we need to approach interactions with power, love, and self-control. That's *responding*. The Greek word for "self-control" doesn't just mean you bite your tongue when you want to say something mean, though it can mean that. What it really implies is responding not from the instability of our emotions but instead from settled confidence of God-given wisdom and discernment. A spirit of power recognizes the authority granted to you in difficult situations by the Spirit of God, not by any power you attempt to snatch back through knee-jerk reactions. And while that all makes good sense, there's a lot of confusion about what it means to remain under a spirit of love in situations like this.

Love does what is in the best interest of another person, but that does not always mean letting them behave as they wish. If you have children, you know that no loving parent gives their kids everything they want! God loves us, but there are always consequences for the choices we make against His will. It's because He loves us that He corrects us. As Hebrews 12:6 says, "The Lord disciplines the one he loves." Love does not hold back consequences; rather, love upholds them for the benefit of the one who needs them in the first place.

John 1:14 says that Jesus "came from the Father, full of grace and truth." Jesus is "full" of saving grace, that through Him we would not receive the punishment we deserve for our sins. But just as much, Jesus is also "full" of truth, that by the Holy Spirit we could have knowledge and discernment of right and wrong.

Full of love. Full of grace. Full of truth. They are inseparable characteristics of God that we are called to grow in as believers and to encourage others to grow in as well. In love, grace means we don't punish, retaliate against, or exact repayment from a person for what they have done. However, in love, we must also commit ourselves to God's standard of right and wrong when it comes to our interactions with others. Consequences are a part of that.

Separating brings up additional consequences in the types of interactions you might have with a person who has abused you. Sometimes you will have to respond by speaking. When a situation requires us to speak, Proverbs 15:1 reminds us to approach the situation peacefully: "A gentle answer turns away wrath, but a harsh word stirs up anger." When you must give verbal responses, be kind and be concise.

Other times, it turns out that no answer is the best response.[9] Jesus silently endured a barrage of false accusations hurled at Him in the hours leading up to His crucifixion. Matthew 27:12–14 says, "When he was accused by the chief priests and the elders, he gave no answer. Then Pilate asked him, 'Don't you hear the testimony they are bringing against you?' But Jesus made no reply, not even to a single charge—to the great amazement of the governor."

Jesus knew there was no point in addressing the charges, not even to defend His good name. A reply would only give credibility to a false claim, so Jesus held to His silence rather than give in to His abusers' games. And don't miss this—Jesus' silence had *power*; through it all the governor was amazed! Silence should not be underestimated; it reveals great strength and self-control.

In the counseling world, these values are expressed in strategies known as "no contact" and "gray rock."[10] "No contact" means eliminating any form of contact with a person for an indefinite period of time. When "no contact" is not possible, for example during shared custody of children, the practice of "gray rock" can be helpful. "Gray rock" treats all communications as logistic and businesslike in nature (or as emotionless as a "gray rock"). Here are other strategies that can help you respond rather than react:

1) Written communication of logistic scheduling details (but not for conversation)
2) Being a "broken record"—offering the same, concise response repeatedly, especially when being baited into a confrontation ("I won't talk to you when you're yelling," or "I understand you disagree, but this is the direction I'm taking.")

Minimizing or eliminating contact is essential to your healing process. A manipulative person will use whatever amount of contact you allow for their benefit, so the fewer words and interactions you share, the better. These methods, when carried out in a spirit of love, are an honorable way to uphold consequences that are intended to free you and allow the Holy Spirit space to work in this person's heart if they are willing to yield. It's a hard thing to do, but it's a very, very good thing to do.

Be aware that your intentions may be misconstrued. People who are well-meaning but don't understand will likely tell you that you are doing the wrong thing. But above all, you are accountable to God, who knows the true motives of your heart. He calls us to do difficult things but always empowers us to do them when they are His will.

Reflection and Prayer

How have your reactions to your abuser been driven by anger or fear? How have you experienced a lack of peace from it? How would you like to respond instead?

In your prayer time, consider asking God what changes in your level of communication are most appropriate for your situation. Ask Him to help you find loving ways to establish boundaries, and pray that He would strengthen you to do difficult things from places of loving wisdom.

SECTION 3

The Healing

The Lord appeared to us in the past, saying:
"I have loved you with an everlasting love;
I have drawn you with unfailing kindness. I
will build you up again, and you, Virgin Israel,
will be rebuilt. Again you will take up your
timbrels and go out to dance with the joyful."

JEREMIAH 31:3–4

The elementary school I attended was run by an ex-nun, though she probably could have passed for an ex-marine.

Before school began each day, students would bound out of cars and onto the play yard, excitedly meeting schoolmates with giggles and glee. But when the morning bell rang, the children would immediately scatter, fearfully scurrying to designated spots beneath the school's flagpole.

The students were expected to line up by class, "silent and straight," in neat, uniform rows arrayed by height. The school principal waited, stone-faced, as she clenched a glinting, silver whistle between her teeth. When line inspections commenced, she'd bellow out orders: "Straighten the line!" or "Stand still!" She'd sternly cajole individual students for wearing mismatched socks or having their shoes untied.

Being the shortest in my class, I usually stood at the front of the line, trembling and avoiding eye contact. I was a nervous chewer; would she notice I'd been chewing on the sleeve of my school sweater? I'd pull my hands up into the sleeves and hold the wadded ends in my hands, hiding the ragged edges until our grade was dismissed to the classroom.

She ran an extremely tight ship, and being the rule-following, stereotypical firstborn that I am, I took every bit of correction and criticism to heart. It wasn't really my school principal's fault, though; throughout my childhood, I can pinpoint specific humiliating experiences that left me sensing that I was deficient and defective. Somewhere in my early elementary years, I figured out that if I presented a perfected, curated version of myself, I could avoid the inevitable devastation my flaws would bring once uncovered.

I earned incredible grades. I earned countless Girl Scout merit badges. If I was in a club or on a sports team, there's a pretty good chance I was the president or captain at some point. During my high school years, I eventually earned more block *W*s than would ever fit on my varsity letterman jacket. I didn't realize it at the time, but I was running so fast because I was running away—from myself. I carried a pervasive fear of worthlessness, and performance was the only way I knew how to relate to God, myself, and the people around me. But I wasn't doing it to feel superior or boost my ego; I simply wanted to "pass inspection," and overdoing was the only way I knew to make up for the anxiety of feeling unwanted.

I'd grown up in church, though the legalistic tradition I was raised under focused more on avoiding the consequences of sin than living in the freedom of grace. God seemed far off and disapproving, which only magnified my sense of shame and valuelessness. I felt as though God tolerated me, and while I believed He loved me enough to save me, I couldn't imagine that He actually delighted in me aside from my efforts to be "my best."

If I'm honest, being consumed with doing "my best" was a deeper symptom of my inability to trust in God. But it wasn't something I chose consciously: the various rejections I experienced early in life created a yearning to belong that even the people closest to me couldn't satisfy. I unknowingly reasoned that if I couldn't rely on the people around me, maybe that meant I was supposed to fight life out on my own.

Despite having garnered a large network of family and friends through all my "doings," I was extremely lonely. In my internal isolation, the enemy began hissing lies to me about God's intentions for my life and my place in the world, just as he did in his gaslighting of Eve. And like Eve, instead of seeking God's best for me, I settled for what I could see and understand on my own. I settled for disloyal friendships, and later toxic relationships, because I could "see the best in people." Plagued by my own inadequacies, it was easy for me to overlook the flaws in others. It seemed to be a gift I possessed, what I was *made* for.

I began to center my worth in portraying the unhealthiest kind of longsuffering. All the while, I was deceived that this was what God had designed me to do and that this suffering made Him proud of me. In the end, I left myself exposed to those who could most easily exploit me as a relatively unguarded target.

Some suffering is foisted upon us, while other suffering is chosen. I've come to understand it's possible to have both kinds simultaneously.

If you'd asked me in my early twenties if I was struggling emotionally, I would have told you I wasn't—or at least not more than the average person. I'd carried the stress of anxiety inside my body for so long it felt completely normal to be in a constant state of alert. But now I know that I'd never really felt safe anywhere—not in my home, in my relationships, or even in my own body. Stillness was frightening, and just as in childhood, performing became my drug of choice when it came to numbing the angst I carried inside my bones.

The most disastrous part of this was that I was constantly applauded for the overachieving that was the clearest sign of my brokenness. What started out with stellar grades and a squeaky-clean reputation morphed into a six-figure career and a jet-setting lifestyle. I dated and married someone who had complementary life ambitions, and while the relationship was always rocky, I chalked it up to the fact that everyone has problems. I pushed through the chaos by pouring myself into my work, and I quickly found success climbing the corporate ladder. I had a couple of kids. Went to grad school. Bought a house. All the things. But the long hours and high-pressure work environment caught up with me as my anxiety skyrocketed. I could no longer ignore the fact that inside, I was spiraling out of control.

My prayers to this point had always been somewhat formulaic, kind of like a to-do list for God. But in this season, my conversations with God became desperate and frantic. I'd suddenly realized I had no idea who God was or if He even existed. I was in ruins. Doubt now tormented me, yet in this utter turmoil my awakening began.

In response to my questioning, God began to gently reveal His love and presence to me. He didn't chastise me; He pursued me, wooed me. He drew me into quiet times with Himself, and I began to discover His character, both on and off the page. It was the sweetest season because, for the first time in my life, I started to feel as though maybe He actually *wanted* me all along.

In Hosea 2:14, God says of His wayward bride, Israel, "I am now going to allure her; I will lead her into the wilderness and speak tenderly to her." I remember reading this verse and suddenly realizing that God had done that for me. My wandering had not been drastic, but subtle; I didn't notice I was veering off course until I needed to call upon a faith I didn't yet have. But God romanced my heart, giving me more of Himself while beckoning me under the banner of His all-consuming grace. In the process, He began restoring pieces of me, and I began to see what He has always seen inside of me.

Looking back, I can now say that season marked the beginning of my awareness of God's redemption of my painful story. Though the rescue from the darkness of my marriage would not occur for another ten years, God knew that I needed to first experience His love for me before I could ever trust Him when He finally parted the raging seas. And He's still alluring me, still calling me to explore the deeper mysteries of His love. In the discovery, He's still showing me more of what He has for me and just how good He truly is.

Isaiah 51:3 says, "The LORD will surely comfort Zion and will look with compassion on all her ruins; he will make her deserts like Eden, her wastelands like the garden of the LORD. Joy and gladness will be found in her, thanksgiving and the sound of singing." God has compassion for our ruins and the devastation abuse has produced. He knows we do not know how to pick up the pieces (or even where to begin). He empathetically approaches us first, offering His tender love as the foundation of the rebuilding of our lives.

Jeremiah 31:3–4 says that before any rebuilding even begins, God draws us to Himself with unfailing kindness. God invites us into His presence, to first experience His gentleness as the healing process begins. That's the hiding place. As we heal, His grace becomes the foundation we return to again and again while our ruins are rebuilt and the transformation of our lives in Him takes shape.

When the Bible speaks of rebuilding and restoration, it's never just to put back what existed. God's view of redemption involves bringing things into alignment with the fullness of glory that He had always intended from the beginning. As we are repaired, God mends our underlying wounds, covers the scars with His grace, and beautifully adorns with joy what once was broken in sorrow. God is on a mission to give back to His children more than what was lost. In this section, we'll explore these precious steps of your own healing journey.

Years into my restoration journey, I can see now that God didn't just want to fix what my marriage had damaged. No, He's too good to do just that much (which would still have been a blessing in its own right). God wanted to redeem an entire lifetime of pain, loneliness, and sorrow, and He worked through my brokenness to capture my heart with a love like I'd never known before. He returned more than what I lost. Finally, in my mind, body, and spirit, I feel more than just safe; I know the joy of what it means to rest because I know I belong.

No doubt your life experiences have informed—or dare I say skewed—your view of God to the point that trusting Him with the unknown seems terrifying. But the beautiful thing I've learned is that God always moves first. He knows how fragile and frightened you are. In His tender and compassionate way, He will gently work with your limitations, healing your wounds and returning what was stolen. During this process, you may experience mixed emotions. You may feel at times that you take two steps forward, only to take one step backward. It may be difficult to understand why the healing process has to unfold this way. Sometimes, demolition is necessary to build something strong and enduring, and God desires that outcome for you. God wants your healing to be complete and long-lasting. As you learn to yield to His restorative work in your life, I pray you can finally revel in the rest that your devoted and doting Father calls you to enjoy.

15

DAD

Because you are his sons, God sent the Spirit of his Son into our hearts, the Spirit who calls out, "Abba, Father."
GALATIANS 4:6

I've heard it said that the way we view God as a Father is often influenced by the relationships we have (or don't have) with our earthly parents and other adult caretakers. Depending on your life experiences, the word *father* can come laced with all kinds of mixed emotions, everything from heartwarming to horrifying.

When you think of your upbringing, did you feel more encouraged or discouraged? Did you feel more accepted or rejected by the adults in your life? Did you feel you could be heard, or were your feelings better kept put away? Wherever you happen to fall on the continuum, your experiences have probably influenced the way you have considered what God is like and what He thinks of you.

Psalm 103:13–14 describes God's nature as Father. It says: "As a father has compassion on his children, so the Lord has compassion on those who fear him; for he knows how we are formed, he remembers that we are dust."

God formed us from dust. He knows how fragile and vulnerable we are. In your human relationships, you may experience vulnerability as a bad thing, a place where you have been hurt, perhaps at the hands of those who were meant to care for you. It's unfair and excruciating, and the experience may have even caused you to resist opening your heart again. Why risk being hurt? But God knows our tender spots so well, and He gently works with us to smooth out the painful knots. Where it can be difficult to bring our vulnerabilities to people, God is able to work through them to teach us we're safe with Him so we can eventually experience His healing safety in communion with others.

God's relationship to us in our refashioning is like that of an artisan to his masterpiece. Isaiah 64:8 says, "You, Lord, are our Father. We are the clay, you are the potter; we are all the work of your hand." If you've ever watched a potter at work, you may have seen that in the molding process they'll patiently form and re-form the clay before firing it. While some of this has to do with getting the shape of the vessel just right, it's also to ensure any imperfections are worked out of the piece before it goes into the kiln to be fired. The artisan knows that any underlying defects will be drawn out in the firing process, leading to fissures and cracks that will ruin the vessel. If necessary, the artist will take a nearly finished piece and start again to preserve the integrity and durability of the piece.

Inevitably, cracks in your understanding of who God truly is and who He has designed you to be will eventually undermine the restoration process you're undergoing now. Your identity is inextricably tied to His, and any false notions you may have about who God is threaten the joy you can experience in understanding who He has made you to be. That is why the healing process can seem so tedious and repetitive, just like a lump of clay being re-formed again and again. You may find yourself at certain points thinking, *Didn't I already deal with this? Why am I feeling triggered again?* As I mentioned before, healing is complex, and it comes in layers. God knows we'd be too overwhelmed to take it all on at once (after all, it's pretty overwhelming as it is). But every layer of healing is meant to take you deeper in your understanding of your underlying weaknesses, to bring you a healing that is increasingly more complete. In the restoration process, God is establishing a new foundation for your life based on His compassionate design for you. And like a careful artist, He'll draw out the beauty and strength in you while kneading out the blemishes at the same time.

To keep you from experiencing God as He is (and therefore knowing yourself as you really are), the devil would have you believe that either you are not a child of God or God is not a good Father. Very often, he uses past neglect and abuse to prove his point; the enemy knows that if you aren't sure where you stand with God, you also can't be sure of how He feels about you or what He truly desires for you. And the enemy would love for you to avoid or reject a relationship with God out of a fear of abandonment, rejection, or unworthiness.

But God is aware of any difficulty you are experiencing in trusting Him, and unlike earthly parents, His faithfulness and commitment to His children is unchanging and everlasting. Deuteronomy 4:31 says, "The LORD your God is a merciful God; he will not abandon or destroy you or forget the covenant with your ancestors, which he confirmed to them by oath." God does not abandon, abuse, or neglect His children. When we are unsure of Him, He remains sure of us. He created you to experience His kindness and tenderness, and He is patient and persistent in the process of drawing you into His love.

What's more, God doesn't want you to approach your relationship with Him as something formal and detached. I think sometimes we think of God as a rigid father, somewhat like Mr. Banks in the movie *Mary Poppins*—not at all playful and requiring perfect etiquette in all our (scheduled) interactions with Him.

But Romans 8:15 says, "You did not receive a spirit of slavery that returns you to fear, but you received the Spirit of sonship, by whom we cry, 'Abba! Father!'" (BSB). Jesus referred to God as "Abba," the equivalent of "Dad" or "Daddy" in our context. This shift in language is important; it implies a relationship that is deeply personalized and affectionate. Dad is the one you can speak plainly to. Dad is the one who knows you've messed up before you even tell Him. Dad is the one who, instead of lecturing you, holds your hand and shows you the right way to go.

It was during my season of deepest brokenness that I felt the Holy Spirit nudge me to refer to God as "Dad" in my prayers. I was puzzled by it, but I found myself awestruck the first time I heard Him whisper *Daughter* to my heart. Knowing how God sees me instills the most sacred sense of childlike wonder, and it brings tears to my eyes when I consider that with Him, I am truly home.

This is the essence of sonship—that we can experience the fullness of relationship with God without the fear of rejection or disapproval we may have become accustomed to in our human relationships. Hebrews 4:16 says that through Christ we can now "approach God's throne of grace with confidence, so that we may receive mercy and find grace to help us in our time of need." You don't need to have it all buttoned up before God. You can approach Him as you are, knowing He eagerly anticipates hearing your voice and fulfilling your needs.

Reflection and Prayer

What feelings does the word *father* draw up for you based on your life experiences? How has this manifested itself in your relationship with God? How have you resisted the re-forming process of healing? How would you like to see that change?

In your prayer time, consider talking to God about the pain that has affected your relationship with Him. Ask Him to show you what it means to consider Him your "Dad" and how you can more fully walk in your identity as His beloved child.

16

RELEASE TO RECEIVE

> Every good and perfect gift is from above, coming down from the Father of the heavenly lights, who does not change like shifting shadows.
>
> **JAMES 1:17**

As you sift through the rubble of your life, it can be very difficult to reconcile the dashed hopes and dreams that lie crushed beneath the wreckage. Memories can become more like nightmares as you start to revisit them through the lens of a truth that you can't now unsee. Nothing is what it seems, whether past or present, and plans you'd made for the future may no longer make sense.

Letting go of the past is challenging, but letting go of the future may be even more daunting. After all, in the grieving process we are expected to move beyond things as they were, even though it's uncomfortable. But releasing a future you thought you were headed toward is both disappointing and disorienting.

During my divorce, I remember lying on my closet floor one evening, staring at the ceiling and wrestling with God about allowing Him to have control of my future. I feared that what awaited me would be just as devastating as what I'd left behind. But the Holy Spirit gently reminded me that what God had for me would be *good*. I'm not talking about good as a measurement—like there's some celestial scale that goes from good to better to best (in which case plain old "good" doesn't really seem all that good). Rather, the understanding that came to me was that "good" defined the intrinsic quality of all God would be composing for me—that if something had to be the fulfillment either of good or of evil in my life, my future would be characterized by goodness. And *that* I could get on board with.

That's the way the word "good" is used in James 1:17 to describe the gifts God has for His children. His gifts are the epitome of goodness, and they descend on us from the throne of heaven. God's gifts are fitting—just what we need at just the right time—and because they come from the hand of a generous Father, they satisfy our needs in ways that imperfect, earthly gifts cannot.

But James makes another important distinction in this verse: he takes the time to deliberately point out that God is unchanging in His generosity. Gift giving can be a very sore spot for abuse victims because abusers often weaponize material goods. Gifts are often given with strings attached, or they are withheld altogether. This can make abuse victims feel leery of receiving gifts or suspicious of the giver's motives. But James wants us to understand that God, unlike the world, is constant and pure in His benevolence.

In Matthew 7:11, Jesus said, "If you, then, though you are evil, know how to give good gifts to your children, how much more will your Father in heaven give good gifts to those who ask him!" In the earliest stages of my healing journey, Jesus' words calmed my anxious heart. He gently reminded me, *If you think you are able to come up with things that are good, wait until you see what I am capable of.*

Even if we can believe God is a giver of good gifts, it's not uncommon to feel disqualified when it comes to receiving them. You may find yourself wondering why God would want to give you anything good. But God's generosity does not hinge on your ability to be "good enough" to receive it. God gives out what is good simply because *He* is good. He is a fountain of goodness—His good gifts are the overflow of His entire nature! He will not hold out on you, and you are not exempt from receiving the good He has been preparing for you since the beginning of time.

God's gifts are not a measurement of how much He loves us but rather evidence that He loves us.

In our suffering, it's often hard to discern the good in the moment. But as Joseph told his brothers in Genesis 50:20, "You intended to harm me, but God intended it for good to accomplish what is now being done, the saving of many lives." Joseph had been sold into slavery, wrongly accused, and imprisoned. Yet with the gift of time his entire perspective of his situation centered on the spiritual gifts, favor, and reputation he received when God eventually delivered him out of his circumstances. God proved Himself both able *and* willing to construct something extremely good out of the ruins of the extremely bad, and He's in the process of doing the same for you.

Reflection and Prayer

Concerning your future, what have you been afraid to trust God with? Has receiving gifts been difficult for you? Do you have trouble believing He wants to give you good gifts? What do you need to release to receive what God has for you?

In your prayer time, consider asking God to teach you more about His goodness. Ask Him to bring to mind the times He has been faithful in the past and to cover you with a sense of hope about the future.

SHAMING THE SHAME

> Looking to Jesus, the founder and perfecter of our faith, who for the joy that was set before him endured the cross, despising the shame, and is seated at the right hand of the throne of God.
>
> **HEBREWS 12:2 (ESV)**

If you've ever wandered through the remains of a dilapidated home, you know that one of the most dangerous objects you'll encounter is broken glass. Old boards and bricks can be pushed aside, but dealing with broken glass requires a different plan (and some protective equipment). And if you show up to such a property without being adequately prepared, your best bet is to try to avoid the jagged fragments altogether.

The shards of a shattered heart are like those fractured panes of glass. Whenever we consider a promise of God or dare to imagine He could truly love us as we are, sometimes something pierces our souls and prevents us from fully grabbing on to that truth. The moment hope begins to arise, discouragement seems to slice through our minds and emotions, allowing doubt to penetrate our growing understanding of who God is and who we are to Him.

The weapon in our wounds that incites all this havoc is shame. Remember that shame differs from guilt in that guilt says, "I made a mistake," but shame says, "I am a mistake." Shame creates that subtle sense that we are too damaged, too burdensome, too deficient, or too much to receive the good that God has. It's the voice that says, "If it does exist, then it's probably not for me."

Shame goes hand in hand with the oppression of abuse and neglect. In Zephaniah 3:19 God says, "I will deal severely with all who have oppressed you. I will save the weak and helpless ones; I will bring together those who were chased away. I will give glory and fame to my former exiles, wherever they have been mocked and shamed" (NLT). Harassment and humiliation are intentional assaults on your sanity and sense of self. Even after an abusive person has been somewhat neutralized, their insidious lies still swirl about you, mocking your every attempt to move on with your life.

The cross is symbolic of the intense shame Jesus confronted through His crucifixion. For sin and death to overtake the Son of God was the ultimate mockery of His perfection and divine power, yet He suffered it on our behalf for the glory and joy that awaited on the other side (Hebrews 12:2).

What I love most about Hebrews 12:2 is the depiction of Jesus' posture toward this shame—He *despised* it. He didn't receive it. He didn't internalize it. Instead, He looked down on it and disregarded it. And if that wasn't enough, Jesus actively insulted and defied the shame by rising up against it through His resurrection, revealing its underlying powerlessness.

You have the *same* power over shame in your own life. But I know shame can be so debilitating that being free of its taunts seems nearly impossible. In Psalm 25, David reveals how to access the power of Christ over shame. He says:

> I trust in you;
> do not let me be put to shame,
> nor let my enemies triumph over me.
> No one who hopes in you
> will ever be put to shame,
> but shame will come on those
> who are treacherous without cause.
>
> Show me your ways, Lord,
> teach me your paths.
> Guide me in your truth and teach me,
> for you are God my Savior,
> and my hope is in you all day long.
> (vv. 2–5)

In this prayer, David reveals that the antidote to shame that has been thrust upon us is hope. But when you feel defeated and hopeless, hope can seem especially elusive (which can lead to feeling even more defeated). In circumstances like these, how can we cut through the shame to find lasting hope?

Psalm 119:114 says, "You are my refuge and my shield; your word is my source of hope" (NLT). We don't have to acquire hope through sheer willpower. You can't think your way out of this with heaps of positivity. Soul-filling hope can pour over us, even in the midst of pain, when we engage in the practice of replacing the lies of shame with God's Word.

I spent decades of my life rehearsing the lies bullies and abusers had spoken over me. Identifying them was one thing, but what was I supposed to believe about myself instead? Exposing the lies you've been believing about yourself is a crucial first step to repairing the wreckage left by shame. But extracting a lie leaves a gaping hole. In spiritual renovation, whenever you take something out, you must put something better in its place.

When you remove the things of the world, fill yourself with the things of the Word.

Learning to replace lies with truth doesn't require you to find the words or to be all that creative. God's already done all the work, and you can simply repeat what Scripture says about you. Do you feel unwanted? God says you are His chosen (1 Peter 2:9). Do you feel worthless? God says you are His masterpiece (Ephesians 2:10 NLT). Do you feel disgusted with yourself because of your past? God says you can forget all that because you are a new creation now (2 Corinthians 5:17).

For every lie, God has a truth you can sit beneath and meditate on. Start with just one verse. Copy it down. Memorize it. Repeat it to yourself when the lies rise up. It's okay if it doesn't sink in at first or if you don't always feel it. God's Word will do the work in you and mend the fractures of your broken heart. And as you practice capturing your thoughts in this way, I pray God's truth will start to make more sense to you than the lies.

Reflection and Prayer

What lies torment and taunt you? Where do these beliefs originate from? What truth do you want to replace these lies with? How do you think it would change your life?

In your time with God, consider talking to Him about the shame you're experiencing and the pain that it causes you. Ask Him to cover you with His comfort and guide you into the truth of who you are to Him.

18

I AM WHO YOU SAY I AM

> To him who is able to do immeasurably more than all we ask or imagine, according to his power that is at work within us, to him be glory in the church and in Christ Jesus throughout all generations, for ever and ever! Amen.
> **EPHESIANS 3:20–21**

As I wandered through the ruins of my own life, I didn't recognize the woman I'd become. I didn't know who I was or what I really enjoyed. Though I presented a confident, polished facade, I felt like a hollowed-out shell of a human. Inside, I'd become a joyless, dreamless drifter, suffering through what seemed to be an endless stream of dreadful tomorrows.

You know that Hillsong Worship song "Who You Say I Am"? I had no idea what that even meant—I did not know who God said I was. Just because you told me I was a child of God did not mean I had any idea what that truly meant to me—or, for that matter, to Him.

Abuse functions by destroying the individuality and God-given uniqueness of the victim. A victim who is crushed by the weight of shame is not able to fully perceive and embrace their own giftedness and will often fear stepping beyond the bounds of what is known to discover the life God has prepared for them. The victim remains caged, impaired, and uncertain, unable to glimpse at the possibility and potential of the unknown.

I was completely out of touch with God's original design for me to the extent that I no longer expected that God would move in my life. Dreams of the future seemed pointless, and desires only increased the sense of longing I already had to endure. Hope was too painful because, at that time, hope seemed to carry a high probability of disappointment. I resolved that it was more spiritual not to have wants or needs, that I should just be happy with my lot and do my best to get by on my own.

Brokenness was no longer my situation; it had become my standard.

But then my marriage imploded. I had no choice but to stare into the face of my brokenness and try to make sense of all the pieces. Life as I knew it was gone, and the inescapable truth was that I had to start over. But where? And even if I knew where to start, where was I going?

During the rebuilding of my wreckage, God revealed that He didn't just want me to know Him; He wanted me to know *me*. He wanted me to understand that the gifts He'd put inside me were parts of Himself and that in enjoying them, I would know more what He is like and what He truly wanted for my life.

It's true that we have to know God to know ourselves. But we can also know ourselves to know God.

First Corinthians 12:6 says, "There are different kinds of

working, but in all of them and in everyone it is the same God at work." God is at work in you, but in ways that may be different from the ways He's working in people around you. Are you creative? That is an element of God as Creator working inside you. Are you compassionate? That's God as Comforter in you. As if you're clay in the hands of the potter, God leaves His thumbprints impressed upon your heart.

Similarly, Romans 12:6 says that "in his grace, God has given us different gifts for doing certain things well" (NLT). This knocked me over when I read it. Do *well*? I began to realize that through my gifts, God had things for me to do and that I had a unique aptitude to do them well. As I grew in my understanding of my gifts, God began to reveal my purpose—and His redemption plan for my pain. In the same way, God has gifted you with unique abilities that will bring forth fantastic new opportunities to fulfill the purpose for which you were created.

In this discovery experience, you can remove the pressure from yourself to figure it all out or get it all right. Philippians 2:13 says, "It is God who works in you to will and to act in order to fulfill his good purpose." God has placed specific qualities in you that He is working to bring to the surface of your awareness. As He works in you, He will bring you inspiration and vision to act in ways that make the most of those gifts and fulfill His purpose for which He placed them inside you. And when that process feels awkward and clumsy, He uses even that to show you more of what He has (or doesn't have) for you; it delights Him that you would open your life to let Him do so. He is the guide, and you are learning to explore the path He is carving out ahead of you.

As I grew to know myself, I finally began to see myself through God's eyes. For the first time in my life, I could have compassion for myself in the face of failures and mistakes. I didn't need to curate a perfected version of myself anymore or beat myself up for my imperfections; I could comfortably settle into my personhood as God had crafted it and, through it, embrace my gifts and limitations.

Eventually God's compassion for me grew into compassion for myself, which extended itself into compassion for others. During this restorative phase of my life, the Holy Spirit illuminated 2 Corinthians 1:4 to me, which says, "He comforts us in all our troubles so that we can comfort others. When they are troubled, we will be able to give them the same comfort God has given us" (NLT). With fresh eyes, I began to realize that God offers us hope for the future born from the devastation of the past. As we learn to lean into that hope, we experience the kind of comfort that allows us to explore the vast unknown that is life. And in that discovery, God reveals more of Himself and His design, which begets even more hope. It might seem crazy to hear me say this, but life can actually become an adventure as our curiosity shifts away from wondering *if* God is working to *where* He is working. As our brokenness yields hopeful expectancy, we cannot help but become hope bearers for the broken souls just behind us.

God's gifts are the gateway by which God reveals so much to us. He works through His creation in us to show us in visual and experiential ways what He is like—even in our own bodies. There's so much goodness in enjoying Him with what He's put inside us. He delivers purpose to our lives, granting us the satisfaction that comes from seeing God at work in our lives, redeeming our pain. In God's hands, your life and your suffering both have meaning. He created you, and He's continually reshaping you to bring you closer and closer to His incredible design for you.

Reflection and Prayer

Have you lost touch with your unique identity? Are you afraid to hope? Are you uncertain about your God-given gifts and purpose? What might you do to explore God's imprint in yourself?

In your time with God, consider talking to Him about hopes and dreams you've been afraid to acknowledge. Ask Him to reveal the special characteristics of Himself embodied in your being and how they connect to living out His purpose and redemption story.

19

VISION AND DIVISION

> I will lead the blind by ways they have not known, along unfamiliar paths I will guide them; I will turn the darkness into light before them and make the rough places smooth. These are the things I will do; I will not forsake them.
> **ISAIAH 42:16**

Healing can be a lonely road. As you grow and gain clarity about the suffering you've endured, you may receive pushback from family and friends who just don't understand.

You might hear things like "You're not doing the loving thing" or "This isn't the Christian way to handle this." And while you would expect to hear this from an abuser, it's crushing to hear it from the people in your life whom you had expected to support you. Family and friends will inevitably have to make a choice in whom they will support, and sometimes that choice will be against you.

Remember the man born blind back in John 9? After the healing, the man got busy elatedly broadcasting about his encounter with Jesus. And despite the fact that they had been witnesses to an obvious miracle, the man's neighbors and the religious leaders remained in denial and disbelief. When Jesus granted the man physical eyesight, He also blessed him with spiritual vision. But the man's ability to see also ended up highlighting the blindness of heart in the people around him.

Jesus told His disciples that their spiritual awakening would reveal who among them was still asleep. In Matthew 10 He said: "Do not suppose that I have come to bring peace to the earth. I did not come to bring peace, but a sword. For I have come to turn 'a man against his father, a daughter against her mother, a daughter-in-law against her mother-in-law—a man's enemies will be the members of his own household'" (vv. 34–36).

As God awakens you to reality, He also begins leading you down a new path. Unfortunately, there will be those who aren't able to follow for one reason or another. For some, this will be temporary; as your healing takes root, they may become curious about what God is revealing through your life—their hearts and minds may open. But for others the division will be permanent if they are deceived and resistant to the truth. You may even experience some backlash or be cut off from certain relationships. Jesus cautions us that this will happen in John 15:21 when He said: "They will treat you this way because of my name, for they do not know the one who sent me."

Whatever the case, do not assume that because you receive pushback it means you're doing the wrong thing. In situations like this, the reactions you witness will reveal the people in your life who are safe to support you, as well as those who are not. Pay close attention.

There is a great grief in this experience. You have already lost a significant relationship and a large portion of life as you knew it. Losing additional relationships is yet another heartbreaking and unexpected consequence of confronting abuse.

But when people turn from you, it's God's intention to bring others to you. When it comes to those who will reject you, Jesus says, "Do not be afraid of them, for there is nothing concealed that will not be disclosed, or hidden that will not be made known. What I tell you in the dark, speak in the daylight; what is whispered in your ear, proclaim from the roofs" (Matthew 10:26–27). In this passage, Jesus explains that we can't convince those who will not listen—that it's God's job to work on their hearts, and He will reveal truth in His time. In the meantime, Jesus' encouragement is to entrust them to God and to turn your attention toward the people God is bringing into your life—people He's already lining up to hear your story.

Psalm 68:6 says, "God sets the lonely in families, he leads out the prisoners with singing; but the rebellious live in a sun-scorched land." As you heal, you will outgrow certain relationships in your life, and the fallout can be frustrating. But God promises not to leave you and to set you into a family of His people who are awake and alive in the truth.

Do you remember me telling you my separation began just weeks after moving across the country? I had *nobody* in my immediate vicinity. No church family, no close friends, no trusted neighbors to lean on. Not a familiar face for hundreds of miles around. But during the earliest months of my healing journey, God miraculously dropped people into my life who understood what I was going through and were very intentional about welcoming me and affirming me. He placed me into a spiritual family of compassionate people who trudged through the muck with me and aided me in becoming more aware of what God was doing in my life. Out of that, I gained a powerful revelation of God's faithfulness and the dearest friends.

There may be moments you feel as though you are standing completely alone. You may even question yourself and wonder how this could ever be the right path. But as you hold to the life-giving truth that is at the core of the restorative work God is doing in your life, you will begin to identify the people God is drawing toward you—the ones He's sent to be His healing hands and feet in your everyday life.

Reflection and Prayer

Have you experienced negative reactions from people in your life about the choices you've had to make relating to your recovery? How has this made you feel? Who in your life has been encouraging and supportive?

In your time of prayer, share with God the disappointments you've felt in the way people have treated you. Ask Him to reveal the safe people He has put in your life and seek Him to surround you with a spiritual family who can nurture you during this season of your life.

20

THE DISCOMFORT OF DELIVERANCE

He says, "Be still, and know that I am God; I will be exalted among the nations, I will be exalted in the earth."
PSALM 46:10

For four hundred and thirty years, generations of Israelites suffered slavery and exile in Egypt (Exodus 12:40). Most were born into captivity. A life of oppression was all they'd ever known. Unbeknownst to them, God was championing for their cause, and in a sudden and unexpected moment, God humbled Pharaoh so he would finally set the Israelites free. Not only that, but in God's rescue of His people He made allowances for them to plunder their enslavers, so they would escape captivity laden with riches.

But in the days and months following their miraculous Red Sea crossing, the Israelites actually found themselves longing once again for the "comforts" of captivity. Freedom was too unfamiliar, and what was once a blessing became a hardship. They rejected the manna God sent to feed them and refused the promised land when they finally arrived. All they could think about was the "easy" life they had before. To us, all this seems unthinkable, but what the Israelites were seeking was the predictable over the preferable. Though the Israelites had been liberated from their captivity in Egypt, their hearts and minds still weren't exactly free.

In the first couple of years that followed the end of my abusive marriage, I have to admit, I wasn't all that different from the Israelites. I pursued relationships that were not good for me, following the same patterns that had led me into a toxic relationship in the first place. But here I was, performing for love like I always had. At the end of another disappointing pseudo-relationship, I knew I couldn't just pass the responsibility on to the men I'd been spending time with. So I asked God, "What am I doing that is keeping me stuck in this pattern?" And He told me, *You don't trust Me.*

And then He gave me Psalm 46:10: "Be still, and know that I am God."

Through coercion and control, abusers manipulate victims into being dependent on them, whether emotionally, financially, socially, or by some other means. But when God breaks those bonds, He invites us to shift our dependence onto Him instead. Giving God the reins of our lives means loosening our grip on the outcomes, and that's really uncomfortable. If I'm being honest, I coped with my own discomfort by leaning on my own understanding and trying to manage things myself. Never has letting go been so hard. Letting God lead stretches what faith you do have and at times may seem to require you to reach a little further than you think you can tolerate. But this part of the healing journey brings greater resilience and the joy of experiencing God's movement in our lives. It's so worth it. But like the Israelites, you have the choice to either participate in the process or resist it.

What the Israelites failed to remember is that God stretches His hand out to us first, to help us learn to stretch our faith out to Him. But this looks different in every situation we encounter. Sometimes, God may ask you to take specific steps of faith, just as He did in instructing the Israelites to walk through the parted waters of the Red Sea. But other times, as with my failed post-divorce relationships, He may be asking you to pause and watch how He will reveal Himself. In either case, we have to learn to wait.

Waiting on God seems to go against our nature. As the problems swirl around us, we may find ourselves tempted—tempted to escape the discomfort, numb the anxiety, or settle for subpar in the name of certainty. But when confronted with what appeared to be certain death, both the Israelites and King David received the same counsel: "Be still."

I know—easier said than done.

Psalm 46:10 says, "Be still." This instruction can be better understood as "stop trying to figure it out" or "stop striving." God's ways are higher than ours, and we are only working with partial information. We don't see everything God sees. When we try to work things out from a position of our own limited understanding, we are bound to get it wrong.

But God sees it all. He sees problems we are not aware of that need to be solved. He sees solutions that our minds cannot conceive of or that we would deem impossible. But when we are still, He says that we will know Him *more* as we watch what He reveals of Himself. When we are still, we cannot take any of the credit for what He does. He unfolds things in such a way that the outcomes would cause us to exclaim, "Only God." God wants us to know He is always working on our behalf, and He's after an awe-inspiring outcome.

The discomfort of deliverance may have you feeling that God has left you or forgotten about you. But Isaiah 41:10 says, "Do not fear, for I am with you; do not be dismayed, for I am your God. I will strengthen you and help you; I will uphold you with my righteous right hand." Panic causes us to look around, scrambling to find ways to make the uneasiness stop. But when anxiety arises, take solace in knowing there's nothing wrong with you; your anxiety is simply calling you to seek safety from the unfamiliarity you are experiencing. Rather than employing quick fixes to escape your anxiety, God invites you to turn to Him in the face of fear to receive comfort and strength.

Tell Him how much this hurts. Tell Him you're afraid to trust Him. Tell Him this is not fair and that you're afraid to mess it all up. In my experience, getting honest with God about my feelings always leads to a profound experience with God's compassion. His compassion for me leads to compassion for myself, and this compassion inevitably yields a renewed confidence that He's got everything in His hands. So whether He asks you to move toward your triggers or watch and wait, you learn to face what is unfamiliar. The discomfort eases, your faith grows, and incrementally you experience more and more freedom in your heart and mind.

You may find yourself wishing you didn't have to learn all these new ways of being. You may get frustrated that you have to do all this work in the first place. It's absolutely appropriate to feel that way. But it's important work with incredible returns, and you are absolutely worth that. New is different, and different can be scary. But when it comes to deliverance, God takes you away from what has oppressed you so He can bless you.

Reflection and Prayer

Do you feel frustrated or overwhelmed when working through all the emotions of the recovery process? What makes you most uncomfortable? Do you feel like you are wandering or like God has abandoned you?

In your time with God, consider telling Him about the difficulties you are experiencing when it comes to trusting Him and His way of doing things. Ask Him for peace in your mind and emotions and for the strength and faith to keep going.

21

ALL THINGS NEW

> "Forget the former things; do not dwell on the past. See, I am doing a new thing! Now it springs up; do you not perceive it?"
>
> ISAIAH 43:18–19

When my rebuilding season began, I couldn't imagine what God could possibly do with a washed-up single mother of three. But as I stood among the shattered pieces of my hopes and dreams, you may remember His gentle encouragement to me: *I'm making all things new.*

This idea of God working out a new thing appears twice in the Bible, at key moments in the salvation story. The first is in Isaiah 43, where God spoke through the prophet Isaiah to foretell the redemption and restoration of His people through the coming of Jesus Christ. To ignite their hope, God first called to mind His mighty deeds at the exodus, reminding them of His power and faithfulness. But shockingly, God then said something unexpected: "But forget all that—it is nothing compared to what I am going to do" (Isaiah 43:18 NLT).

A similar phrase appears again in the book of Revelation: "He who was seated on the throne said, 'I am making everything new!' Then he said, 'Write this down, for these words are trustworthy and true'" (21:5). In this vision, Jesus declared that through Him and in His second coming, all things would finally be completely renewed. And while this phrase gives us hope as we look toward eternity, we should understand that God is also *already* redeeming things in our everyday lives as we step more fully into forever.

Looking at the past can be helpful—if it draws us to remember God's faithfulness and inspires us to take what has happened and use it as fuel to move forward. But we can't get stuck staring at what is behind any more than we can drive down the freeway by looking in the rearview mirror. We're not going that way. Instead, God invites us to develop a habit of fixing our eyes on the horizon ahead, and He beckons us to begin looking for the new things He is already unfolding in our midst as He carries us into redemption and the future. God wants you to start *expecting* Him to do something pretty great, because He's already proving it.

When we've been hurt, it can be hard to expect anything other than disappointment. We think small thoughts and pray small prayers. But perceiving what God is up to will challenge you to stop looking for what's reasonable and step into the realm of the impossible. Habakkuk 1:5 says, "Look at the nations and watch—and be utterly amazed. For I am going to do something in your days that you would not believe, even if you were told."

Psalm 37:4 says, "Take delight in the LORD, and he will give you the desires of your heart." Does this mean you'll get everything you want? Well, not exactly—some of our hearts' desires are not actually good for us, and God knows that. Through some serious disappointments, God revealed to me that certain things I had desired were actually birthed from insecurity and anxiety. Had He given me what I wanted, He would have been allowing me to build a house that could not withstand the storms of life. Instead, He responded to the longings beneath those desires, granting me the security and peace I really needed. In effect, He changed the desires of my heart and replaced them with new hopes and dreams rooted in righteousness.

God is so good to give us what we don't even know we need.

God is at work redeeming the past, the present, *and* the future, all at the same time. We're not just putting in our time, waiting for Him to show up in some far-off, distant future. The future is unfolding right now, in ever-increasing measure. Psalm 27:13–14 says, "I remain confident of this: I will see the goodness of the Lord in the land of the living. Wait for the Lord; be strong and take heart and wait for the Lord." If you are alive, congratulations; you are in the land of the living! You can take heart knowing that God wants you to experience His goodness in the here and now as He leads you into the pleasures that await you in the future.

It's not either-or. It's both-and.

Your life, your pain, your desires—they all matter to God. They are the offering from which He constructs your new life and future. Trust that He desires to multiply the offering like the loaves and fishes, and patiently wait on Him to see what He can do. Keep offering, keep praying, keep seeking, and remain confident of this: "He who began a good work in you will carry it on to completion until the day of Christ Jesus" (Philippians 1:6).

Reflection and Prayer

Have you had difficulty believing God can make something good out of all you've endured? How have you been thinking small, expecting disappointment? How would your thoughts and prayers change if you approached God with hopeful expectation?

In your prayer time, consider telling God about the doubts you have about your future. Lay out your desires before Him and ask Him to help you understand what it means to be open to His will while remaining expectant. Ask Him to bring you the patience to wait on Him, and thank Him for the work He is already doing to make all things new.

NOTES

1. Lawrence Kasdan, George Lucas, and Philip Kaufman, *Indiana Jones and the Raiders of the Lost Ark,* directed by Steven Spielberg (Paramount Pictures, 1981).

2. L. T. Mega, J. L. Mega, B. T. Mega, and B. M. Harris, "Brainwashing and Battering Fatigue: Psychological Abuse in Domestic Violence," *North Carolina Medical Journal* (Sep–Oct, 2000), 61(5): 260–5. PMID: 11008456, https://pubmed.ncbi.nlm.nih.gov/11008456/.

3. Kate Cavanagh, R. Emerson Dobash, Russell P. Dobash, and Ruth Lewis, "Remedial Work: Men's Strategic Responses to Their Violence against Intimate Female Partners," *Sociology*, 35(3) (2001), 695–714.

4. *Cambridge Dictionary*, s.v. "Smear campaign," accessed December 7, 2021, https://dictionary.cambridge.org/us/dictionary/english/smear-campaign.

5. "Nest Building Facts," JourneyNorth.org, accessed December 7, 2021, https://journeynorth.org/tm/eagle/annual/facts_nest.html.

6. *Online Etymology Dictionary*, s.v. "Compassion," accessed December 7, 2021, https://www.etymonline.com/word/compassion.

7. Steven Lampley, "Hoovering and the Narcissistic Victim," *Psychology Today*, March 24, 2020, https://www.psychologytoday.com/us/blog/captivating-crimes/202003/hoovering-and-the-narcissistic-victim.

8. Sharie Stines, "Narcissistic Abuse Recovery: Healing from the Discard," *PsychCentral*, October 16, 2019, https://psychcentral.com/pro/recovery-expert/2019/10/narcissistic-abuse-recovery-healing-from-the-discard#4.

9. Gary Thomas, *When to Walk Away: Finding Freedom from Toxic People* (Grand Rapids, MI: Zondervan, 2019).

10. Crystal Raypole, "Dealing with a Manipulative Person? Grey Rocking May Help," *Healthline*, December 12, 2019, https://www.healthline.com/health/grey-rock#offer-nothing.

Made in the USA
Middletown, DE
31 October 2022